Sacred Dung

Grace to Turn Bad Things Into Good Things

John D. Duncan

Austin Brothers Publishing
Fort Worth, Texas

[Handwritten inscription:] Dre Thii you, ministry, encouragement, and the positive difference you make in people's lives and, for God's Kingdom — Blessings, Psalm 91, John

Sacred Dung:

Grace to Turn Bad Things Into Good Things

by John D. Duncan

ISBN 978-0-9964285-4-5

Published by Austin Brothers Publishing

Fort Worth, Texas

www.austinbrotherspublishing.com

Printed in the United States of America

This and other books published by Austin Brothers Publishing can be purchased at www.austinbrotherspublishing.com

Contents

Foreword

In 2009, the Country band, Sugarland, released a hit song titled, *It Happens*. The refrain of the chorus reverberates an ancient question posed by Job and his friends, "Why do bad things happen?"

Ain't no rhyme or reason
No complicated meaning
Ain't no need to over think it
Let go laughing
Life don't go quite like you planned it
We try so hard to understand it
Irrefutable, indisputable
Fact is pssh
It happens.

John Duncan takes this ancient question head on, and provides encouragement for your journey. John has been my pastor, colleague, and friend for almost 20 years. Through the years (using a phrase from another song), I've witnessed John's remarkable ability to deal with challenges in life. Whether it was supporting his wife and family through cancer, ministering to a grieving family and church over the tragic death of a teenager, receiving verbal abuse by critical church members, or leading a growing church, John responds each time with resilient grace.

Shortly after our daughter discovered she had breast cancer, a woman told her, "Someday you'll see cancer as a blessing." Our married daughter replied, "Never." At the age of twenty-nine and yet to have children, cancer was not in her life plan. But dung happens. It's not a question of if, but when.

Eight years after this life-changing revelation, our daughter is a mother of two healthy children. Though scarred from multiple surgeries, she chose to NOT let cancer define her. Instead, she used her illness as a launching pad for exploring God's incomprehensible love. (Ephesians 3:19) She now understands on a spiritual level what the woman meant: "Someday you'll see cancer as a blessing." Like Job, our daughter's sorrow turned to joy, and her fear into faith. As John Duncan writes in this book, "You put the past in your rearview mirror, open your heart to God's wonderful surprise, and reach forward by His grace as you journey onward. New commitments spell new goals, new dreams, and necessitate the unfear of taking risks."

You or someone close to you may right now may be wading in the pain of life. This book is for you. It is time for you to put the past behind and use it as an opportunity for growth and healing.

God never wastes our pain, suffering, or experiences. Your greatest contributions to others will come through your weaknesses and hurts. Tolle writes, "Life is not a packaged tour, but an adventure." The best trips occur when you go off road and get in the muck and the mire—the dung of life. The best stories are about overcoming difficulties. What will yours be?

As you read this book, use the following spiritual practices to guide your journey.

1. Write out your timeline listing the highpoints and low points of your life. What are some significant spiritual highlights? Where did you feel far away from God?

What valleys are you currently experiencing? Looking back with eyes of faith, where do you see God's presence during those difficulties? How did God bring you through them? Celebrate God's compassion for you, even in times of lament. (Lamentations 3:20-24)

2. Take an inventory of the wounds in your life. Make a list of places and relationships that need healing. Like Job, cry out to God about your suffering. Then be still and let God speak into your heart. Seek out someone with whom you feel comfortable to pray with and for your inner healing.

3. Keep a journal of your thoughts and feelings during your reading. Write quotes from the book and scripture passages that come to mind. Before you read, ask God to speak to your through this writing.

4. Write your story of sacred dung. Tell your story of how sorrow was turned to joy, your loss to gain, and your hurt to healing. Share your story with family and friends. Maybe you are currently knee

deep in difficulties. Write how you'd like, by faith, for the story to end.

Embrace the sacred dung in your life. Use it to rejoice, to grow, and to help others.

Dr. Daryl Eldridge
President of Rockbridge Seminary

Introduction

I solved one puzzle in my life. It took me years to outline the frame, pick the right pieces, and handle the wrong pieces of the puzzle enough to help put the right pieces into place. I figured it out, but it took years. I woke up one morning after oversleeping, thinking I was late for work, but then realized there was no place to go to work. Suddenly, I remembered, "You're a wildcatter looking for an oil well; an open spring flowing with endless water that only needs a field; and what the experts call a 'freelancer,' a freelance writer, your own boss."

Mixed with hope and despair of living out my dream, I wiped the sleep out of my eye, shed a single tear from the left corner of my right eye, and rolled over into a sea of pillows, alone, confused, and wondering, "What just happened?" Then it hit me. It was this brilliant thought that took me years to discover. Here it is. Please do not laugh. Here it is: bad things happen.

The more I pondered this deep thought the more I began to flip the phrase around. Bad things happen to good people. Good things happen to bad people. Bad things happen to bad people. Good things do happen to good people, too. But mostly, stuff happens, planned and unplanned, days when you stand at the window and feel the sunshine and glory of hope when suddenly the house shakes, the curtains fall, the electricity shuts down, and you stare at a huge crack in the wall from the floor. See, bad things happen. There. That's the end of the story. Or is it?

Write this down: Three things you can expect in life: failure at your doorstep, good people do bad things, and bad things happen to good people. Since I am not a pessimist and live quite optimistically, I want to begin to turn your thoughts in a more positive direction. Learn to laugh through

failures, bless these who curse you, and praise God for bad things and trials.

When I attended seminary I had two jobs: I worked at a Christian bookstore and I helped manage apartments. The good news showered me with an introduction to literature while I worked at the bookstore. My job as apartment manager delivered some bad news. The bad news included collecting the rent even if people refused to pay, mowing the lawns in the Texas heat, and cleaning out refuse, garbage, and trash. The landlord evicted one angry tenant. The landlord also asked me to deliver the sad news to the delinquent tenant. The furious tenant decided he would trash the apartment, spread trash around, and leave me a horrific gift of moldy food, melded jars, and a mess with a stench of foul odor like dung for me to clean. I cleaned and gagged until the job was complete. In this book we will learn that sacred dung requires clearing out and cleaning out to move forward in life minus the gagging.

Consider the woman who walks her dog in the neighborhood. She leashes her dog, waltzes through the neighborhood, the dog stops to do his business, and a beautiful red cardinal captures the dog owner's attention. She stares at the bird and steps in dung, dog mess that makes her new white tennis shoes look like they have been smeared with mud. The good news was the woman would have green grass in that spot, the dung working as nutrients to fertilize her yard. The bad news is the dung crust and the dung smell had to be shoveled from her shoe. In this book we will learn that scared dung provides fertilizer that supplies a resource for future days.

Or think of a woman who has colitis, stomach trouble that upsets her rest pattern, creates pain in her belly, and worry in her mind. She visits her physician, who refers her to a specialist who diagnoses her problem and prescribes a medicine for healing. The medicine prescribed, although unadvertised, provides nutrients for healing, but part of the healing elements include fecal matter, dung. In this book we will learn that sacred dung works in us to heal the unsettled, painful, and broken parts of our lives.

Not long ago I met a friend at a restaurant in Austin, Texas. He wore a sport coat, jeans, and cool shoes. If you knew him, you would think he appears as an average guy. In truth my friend Jason lives as no average guy. Actually, he feels fortunate to breathe, even walk or sing, which he likes to do.

He shared his testimony over Mexican food on a day filled with sunshine and hope. I had heard his testimony before, but he gave it to me again because he loves to share his God story. He always begins with this simple sentence, "I should have died twice, so I know there is something amazing that I am called to do." You can find his story online at jasonblacklive.org. What is Jason's story?

Before I tell you Jason's story, I need to tell you that he sings in the opera. His voice booms. His vibrato rattles the glass. When he sings, people listen. I know this because, right smack dab in the middle of lunch while I ate my chicken fajitas wrapped in a corn tortilla, Jason shared his story, felt the excitement of God's grace, and started singing. The louder he sang, the more I slouched in my chair. All eyes at the restaurant moved to our table, to us. "Jason, people are staring at us," I said as he smiled a devilish smile and apologized if he had embarrassed me. Jason sings the amazing grace of God with an amazing voice.

Jason will tell you he thrives as a walking miracle. On March 14, 1999, Jason and his fiancé, Tausha, had just finished the opera, started home on the highway in his GEO Storm, and faced a split-second decision: avoid nearby pedestrians or move toward a solid concrete wall where shockingly sat an unlit, wrecked vehicle in the fast lane. Within seconds Jason and Tausha crashed. She broke an arm, had a concussion, and her body bled from cuts.

Her injuries appeared minor compared to Jason's. Trained rescue workers wielded their Jaws of Life to cut Jason out of the car. Workers stood shocked in disbelief when Jason survived the wreck. Jason told me at lunch how doctors, medical personnel, and professionally trained experts delivered the news in the aftermath of his wreck. "If you recover at all, it will take two years," they said.

Jason shared with me how the head trauma caused behavioral disorders, craziness, and made him unrecognizable to family, friends, and Tausha. Jason also broke numerous bones in his body. Jason tells the story with a grin, somewhat hilariously how doctors *institutionalized* him, how they informed him he might not recover, and how he started healing quickly, started walking, talking, and miraculously recovered to sing again.

The lead tenor recovered, married the soprano, Tausha, and life swung from hopelessness and despair to joy and wonder. Before long the opera singer who thought he might never sing again, sang on the stage and around the world.

In 2001, Jason and Tausha planned to move into a new home. Moving day came and Jason solicited the help of two strong, robust, and eager teenage boys to assist in moving boxes, furniture, and belongings. While lifting and moving a large six-foot glass table, Jason at one end and one of the teenage helpers at the other end, the table slipped out of the teenager's hand, hit the ground, and sliced like a knife into Jason's neck.

As only Jason can describe it, the glass crashed down on his neck like a guillotine, cut a deep gash in his neck from his ear lobe to his chest nearly decapitating him, nicked his spine, sliced a jugular vein, and shredded his voice box. Jason had the presence to dial 911, was rushed to the hospital, lost a tremendous amount of blood, and survived to whisper to ER doctors that he was an opera singer. Doctors later explained the severity of the cut vocal cord, the slim odds of his ever talking normally again, and the sad news of his non-existent chances of singing again. Recovery came slowly, painfully, and quietly, the opera singer pondering his future without a voice.

After six weeks in shock and surprise, Jason started talking with a simple *hello*. The rest is history. Jason credits the twice-miraculous recoveries to the grace of God. He also confessed to me that before the first accident he had not lived for God, but that now he is all-in-for-God. Christ serves as both his reason for being and reason for singing. Tausha admits that faith and love won the day to help their friendship, marriage, and lives win the day.

Can you imagine surviving through two accidents like Jason did? One day you wake up in the dung of despair wondering if you will ever be normal again. Another day you find yourself in a pool of blood in the stench of the dung of disaster and tearfully long to sing loud your joy when doctors inform you that you might not ever again hear your own whisper. And to think of Tausha, family, friends, and fellow singers wishing the nightmare would end, the despair could be tossed like the trash, or the disaster could be wiped away like dung on your shoe, or be cured with a pill laced with excrement.

Whatever life delivers, rest assured sometimes you step into bad stuff; at other times it falls into your lap and, still worse, it shocks you in the agony of unexpected pain.

Jason's struggle, trauma, and drama led him to find ways to turn the bad things into good things. The singer renewed his purpose in singing. The once-upon-a-time voiceless opera singer found his voice again and learned afresh to listen to God's voice. The booming-voiced tenor rejoiced to sing shamelessly, victoriously, and joyfully in rehearsals, on stage, and, of all places, in restaurants with a friend. Write this down: bad things happen. Ponder this: can bad things turn into good things?

Before I delve deeper into this book, and before you continue reading, I must supply three disclaimers. First, no one plans for bad things to happen and, honestly, not all bad things turn into good things. Some bad things stay bad and you learn to overcome the bad with the good. Not everybody receives a miracle like Jason, but rather most people have to wrestle with and travel through the bad thing.

Second, in writing this book, I offer hope more than two-step or four-step prescriptions of "do this and here's how it will turn out good." Doctors supply prescriptions and I only offer hope as the medicine that supports a life of joy in Christ.

Third, I never dreamed I would ever write a book using a four-letter word. However, dung revels as a biblical word used in the Bible, by ancient philosophers, and by ancient doctors as a routine part of life: something to throw out; something to smear in the soil of the soul like fertilizer; and something to digest for healing. Anyway, I never dreamed of using such a word until one day I searched Paul's use of the word dung in Philippians 3:

> *"Yea doubtless, and I count all things but loss for the excellency of the knowledge of Christ Jesus my Lord: for whom I have suffered the loss of all things, and do count them but dung, that I may win Christ, and be found in him, not having mine own righteousness, which is of the law, but that which is through the faith of Christ, the righteousness which is of God by faith: That I may know him, and the power of his resurrection, and the fellowship of his sufferings, being made conformable unto his death; If by any means I might attain unto the resurrection of the dead. Not as though I had already attained, either were already perfect: but I follow after, if that I*

may apprehend that for which also I am apprehended of Christ Jesus. Brethren, I count not myself to have apprehended: but this one thing I do, forgetting those things which are behind, and reaching forth unto those things which are before, I press toward the mark for the prize of the high calling of God in Christ Jesus" (Philippians 3:8-14, KJV).

Did you see that? Paul addresses putting the past behind like throwing out the trash. Paul encourages transforming power and fellowship with Christ in [His] suffering like turning dung into fertilizer. Paul challenges you to reach for the goal of God's highest, best, and most glorious—like joy as a medicine.

In Greek, the word dung is *skubalon*, a neuter noun that knows no difference between male or female, Jew of Greek, or another human being. Dung hails as excrement, a normal part of life's routine whether you are a human being, an animal, an apartment manager cleaning out the trash, a woman walking your dog, a medical worker, or a victim of life's bad circumstances that stink.

If you read the apostle Paul or Jesus for that matter, or the prophet Ezekiel, or even Nehemiah, you will discover that dung, in spite of what you might think, does possess redeeming qualities. Detestable dung might waltz into your life as something bad, but end up as something good. Furthermore, dung might prove sacred in the sense of God's blessing when filtered through His sifter of grace.

I titled the book *Sacred Dung* to make my sacred book series a trilogy matching *Sacred Space* and *Sacred Grit*. The concept of sacred dung involves God's grace at work in your life to turn bad things into good things. *Sacred Space* invites you to nail your heart to the sacred work of God in Christ by the Holy Spirit. *Sacred Grit* allows that faith in Christ helps you push through when you feel like giving up. Life itself illumines with mystery in awe of the sacred. Life takes us on a journey no less winding and twisting and full of hills and valleys than it is sacred. Along the way, unexpected, unavoidable, even unwelcome events interrupt, and in some cases, attach to our lives like a leech trying to suck the blood and life out of us. How do we respond? How will you respond? So many times we miss the sacred on our journeys.

If you look up sacred in Latin, the gamut runs wild from *sacra* or *sacer* (sacred) to sacerdotalis (priestly) to *sacramentum* (an oath and guarantee or deposit of money in a lawsuit) to *sacrarium* (shrine, chapel, sacred place) to *sacrificium* (sacrifice) to *sacrilegium* (sacrilege; temple robbing, violation of sacred rites). What is sacred requires value, a pledge or oath to its value, and a sacrificial element, holding nothing back if you will, giving your all to it, as if your life depended on it. To violate or to demonstrate violence toward the sacred proves sacrilegious, a kind of temple robbing, and definite violation of sacred rites.

In antiquity, the Roman concept of *sacra* combined two ideas: first, in a religious sense of homage to a god or family sacred rites, an oath or pledge, especially in honor of burial for a relative; two, in a legal sense, *sacra* later connected to Roman law in legal inheritance, legal rights passed from one generation to the next. In a religious sense in antiquity, Romans pledged to their god or deity by giving up something or removing something from their presence like a bull, piece of bread, cake, or wine. The sacrifice ("to make sacred") was then made to the god on the altar by sacrificing the bull, leaving the bread at the altar, placing the cake on the altar, or pouring the wine over the altar. A religious act involved a sacred act.

If you look up dung in the dictionary, well, I think you do not need a dictionary. Step in it. Smell it. Feel it, and mud comes to mind. Dung, though, possesses qualities necessary for Christian growth. And that is what I will explore in this book, Sacred Dung. The Apostle Paul's life revolving around Philippians will assist us on his journey and ours.

We will explore sacred refuse in chapter one. Each person in life needs a dung gate, a place to throw out the trash. How does this work in the stench and apparent disaster of our lives?

Chapter two will leads us to the importance of a sacred refrain. Consider a farmer, farming, and dung as a fertilizer to help you grow for and blossom for future days. Can we take the nasty stuff that life dumps on us and plow it deep in the soul for future days? Can we spread dung like manure over our hearts, figuratively speaking, and allow it to fertilize the soul so as to equip our lives for future ministry? A wilderness experience might await you.

Chapter three empowers sacred dung as a source for sacred refuge. The hurts in our lives must find a measure of healing before we can effectively serve Christ and others. How can we trust God again? How can dung help us see the good in the bad things?

Write this down: bad things happen. Turn the page and begin the adventure of seeking God's face and asking God to turn bad things into good things for His glory. Turn the page and stumble into sacred dung. Turn the page and start looking for one thing everybody needs: a dung gate. Turn the page and move from the past toward the future, from the wilderness to hopefulness, and from hurt to healing. Turn the page. Go ahead. I assure you dung is not always what you think.

But what things were gain to me, those I counted loss for Christ. Yea doubtless, and I count all things but loss for the excellency of the knowledge of Christ Jesus my Lord: for whom I have suffered the loss of all things, and do count them but dung, that I may win Christ... (Philippians 3:7-8, KJV).

Sacred Refuse

From past to future

"The leaves are falling, falling as from far,

as though above were withering farthest gardens;

they fall with a denying attitude.

And night by night, drown into solitude, the heavy
earth falls far from every star.

We are all falling. This hand's falling too – All have
this falling-sickness none withstands.

And yet there's One whose gently-holding hands

This universe's falling can't fall through."

~Ranier Maria Rilke, Autumn[1]

Write this down: Everybody in life at one time or another needs a dung gate.

Three things I must tell you. Once I got stuck in the mud that smelled like dung. Two, pigeons once dropped dung on my head. Three, I am very good at taking out the trash.

Sometimes in life people get stuck. Of their own making or because of circumstances beyond their control, people wake up and find themselves stuck in a place or a job or a relationship or a mental or spiritual roadblock.

Once, while helping a friend move, rain began to fall from the sky. In Texas where I live, we say in a moment like that, "It's raining cats and dogs." While rain poured onto the house, onto the men moving furniture, and onto the furniture, I advised my friend, "Move the truck closer." The truck had double back tires, glowed with yellow while pasted on the side black letters named *Ryder* blurred beneath the hard rain. The truck, I am

---

1 Rainer Maria Rilke, Rilke: *Poems* (New York: Alfred A. Knopf, 1996), 20.

sure, weighed more than the ten men moving furniture combined.

"The truck will get stuck if we move it," my friend said as water dripped from his nose while his green shirt soaked water and his infectious smile provided sun underneath the dark clouds.

"No it won't. Just try it. Move the truck. Come on. You can back it up closer to the door so your furniture will not get wet," I urged with ingenuity.

My friend climbed up in the truck, backed it up, and almost immediately the back wheels spun, dug a mud hole, and found themselves, along with the yellow truck, stuck in the mud. One broken chain and one powerful truck chained to the Ryder truck later and the truck was unstuck. However, during the hour or so while we worked to free the truck, I noticed that I smelled mud which in turn smelled about as good as a cat's litter box, or like a pig farm when the wind blows out of the south and you're standing on the porch of your house to the north. Sometimes people get stuck in the dung.

At other times, the dung drops down on us shockingly, surprisingly, and suddenly. Once when I attended an NBA Dallas Maverick basketball game, dressed to the nines, as they say, in my *best dress like Dallas clothes* while walking from my car to the arena, I passed under trees in the electricity of spring. The sun was high in the air. A wisp of cloud painted a picture on the canvas sky as if the Second Coming might happen at any minute. Birds chirped. Excitement swelled in the air as well as in my heart because any time I can attend an NBA basketball game makes my heart sing the happy song.

Shockingly, surprisingly, and suddenly as I walked under a blooming tree, a pigeon deposited last night's supper directly on my head. Instinctively, I reached for the warm spot I felt on my head, noticed white on my blue shirt, and greenish junk that looked like nasty snot on my jeans. I do not have to tell you what happened. If it's true that birds of a feather flock together, it's equally true that when a bird lifts its feathers, cover your head or run for cover or carry an umbrella for days when the rain pours or when pigeons decide to rain on your parade. And so my point: sometimes the dung falls on you when you least expect it.

If you visit my house and we share a meal, we might eat a delightful meal, clean the table and dishes, and then, I can assure you, I will take out the trash. Trash stinks no less than mud or cat litter or a pig pen, and as much as bird deposits on your head. I do not like for the trash to pile up to stink for the company, or to overrun the kitchen. Believe me, I am a highly skilled take-out-the trash kind of person. Like Jesus separating the sheep and the goats, I separate the regular trash of food scraps and paper wrappers and ice cream buckets and Popsicle sticks and cans and cracker boxes from the recyclable items such as newspapers, plastic jugs, and Ozarka water bottles.

Mottoes ring in my ears: "reduce, reuse, recycle, and refuse" help provide a healthier environment. Save the whales! Save the seals! Save the birds! We often hear such advertisements as they remind us of working together to keep a healthier and cleaner environment. I do not think it is a bad idea. We should all do our part. And this is why everybody needs a dung gate: to reduce, reuse, recycle, and-of course-discard the refuse. Undiscarded refuse can turn into a real household problem.

Refuse can stack up in our souls, too; stuff that gets us stuck in the mud; stuff that falls into our lives shockingly, surprisingly, and suddenly; and stuff that stacks up in the soul and stinks. Everybody needs a dung gate.

If you study the history of Israel, especially Nehemiah's rebuilding of the broken-down walls of Jerusalem, you will find that you could walk near the walls and count numerous potential gates. In Nehemiah's day, the gates provided openings or doors or passageways for people to enter or leave the city. Nehemiah mentions a specific gate riding on his horse late at night, inspecting the breached walls of Jerusalem, and arriving at the south wall on the southwest corner of the section that had been destroyed by fire. He refers to the gate as *Dung Gate* (Nehemiah 2:13).

Later we hear of a man named Malkijah who rebuilt the gate, put doors on it, and attached bolts and bars on the doors. Malkijah means *my king is Jehovah*, and he served as a ruler of Beth Hakkerem, a chief district of the city. The man whose king was Jehovah repaired the Dung Gate because it proved pivotal as a place to rid the city of refuse and trash.

Beyond the gate sat the Valley of Hinnomor, more properly, the Valley of the Son of Hinnom, if you prefer Aramaic. Hinnom served as a boundary line for two Israelite tribes: Benjamin to the north, Judah to the south. Who owned the land? One can only guess Hinnom and later his son; but general thinking seems that the land became a trash heap, a dumping ground, and a place for refuse. Historically, human sacrifices offered to the god Molech took place at Topheth, a city in the Valley of Ben Hinnom, "where they burned incense on the roofs to all the starry hosts and poured out drink offerings to other gods" (Jeremiah 19:13). As time progressed, the valley became associated with child sacrifice, divination, witchcraft, and evil (2 Chronicles 33:6). Jeremiah lamented the region as "the Valley of Slaughter" (Jeremiah 19:6).

If you prefer the Greek name attached to the Hebrew name of the Valley of Hinnom, *Gehenna* as it is transliterated into Greek, you need look no further than Jesus who used his lips to utter the word eleven times. James used it once to refer to the evils of the tongue like the spokes of a chariot wheel catching on fire and sizzling through the spokes to the outer wooden rim and wrecking the chariot (James 3:6). The image hails as a destructive one. Judging Jesus' use of the word, and his half-brother James' use of *Gehenna*, the word translates as hell, and swirling around it images of fire and smoke, and a resting place for refuse, trash, unrelenting fools, rebellious sinners, and

self-righteous Pharisees acting as kindling, like firewood for the glowing fire.

If all this sounds scary, and even as you read, the stench of black smoke and burnt toast in the toaster affects your mind and causes you to imagine *Gehenna* as a bad place, an evil place, a fiery place, and a dumping ground, it is. Jesus painted *Gehenna* as the refuse just beyond the door of the Dung Gate where all the bad stuff goes in the end, the final judgment, the day when Christ holds the scorecard and/or video replay at the end. Please do not send me letters or an email; this book announces the grace to turn bad things into good things, but never forget that in life, and sometimes in death, yes, write this down: bad things happen. They really do. Grace happens, too.

This dung discussion and picture of the Dung Gate with its swinging doors and stench beyond the walls leads us to the Apostle Paul. The tent-making apostle wrote a letter from prison in Rome to the Christians at Philippi. Paul made a stop by the River Gangites to give witness to Christ on his second missionary journey. Roman law provided safety nets for prayer gardens known as *proseuche* where Jews often prayed.

A prayer garden near the River Gangites set the scene where Paul met a wealthy woman from Thyatira named Lydia. Her wealth centered on her business acumen, a manufacturer and seller of purple. Her wealth afforded her the privilege of buying a large home. When she met Paul, she may have known Philippi, its history of royalty when Philip II, the King of Macedon, renamed the city of Krenides after himself in 356 B.C., hence Philippi.

Krenides hints at the city's beauty with it wells, waters, and *springs*. The city was set in the hills, constructed after a small-scale Roman city with an arch, a forum, an acropolis, and a *bema*, judgment bench. Lydia may have known Philippi's vast riches from days past when gold mines emptied themselves of gold, and miners lined their pockets with richness from the nearby mines. Lydia may have known Philippi's bloody history when Roman general and statesman Antony and his ally Octavian defeated Brutus and Cassius in the infamous battle of Philippi in 42 B.C. Lydia walked through the streets of Paul's day knowing of a trade route as the main thoroughfare like any highway today, knowing of its porticoes, library, theater, monuments, fountains, agora or marketplace (think of an open-air Wal-Mart) and two temples towering over the city. Lydia also knew prayer as she routinely ventured to the *proseuche* by the River Gangites to pray.

It makes you wonder if Paul, writing in Rome, closes his eyes and takes a trip in his mind, walking through the city, watching the sun set and radiate the waters over the river as the birds fly overhead, and as the sun's rays sparkle on the water; if maybe he recalled Lydia, praying at the prayer garden; if maybe he remembered the day Christ came into her life; if maybe this led him to write about prayer. It makes you wonder if the imprisonment, the threat of Roman power to Christianity in Philippi, and his love for Lydia and the saints in Philippi, no less his love for prayer, led him to pen these words: "And this is my prayer: that your love may abound more and more in knowledge and depth of insight, so that you may be able to discern what is best and may be pure and blameless until the day of Christ, filled with the fruit of righteousness that comes through Jesus Christ—to the glory and praise of God" (Philippians 1:9-11, NIV).

It makes you wonder if Paul wrote late into the night, the sound entering his ears of the chariot wheels rolling through town like eighteen-wheel trucks carrying their transport goods and caravan wares. It makes you wonder if Paul wrote wearily, warily, prayerfully agonizing over his life or death and then scratched out these words: "Rejoice in the Lord always. I will say it again: Rejoice! Let your gentleness be evident to all. The Lord is near. Do not be anxious about anything, but in everything, by prayer and petition, with thanksgiving, present your requests to God. And the peace of God, which transcends all understanding, will guard your hearts and your minds in Christ Jesus" (Philippians 4:4-7, NIV). It makes you wonder if Paul smelled the dung in prison while he wrote, if maybe he mentioned *rejoice* because rejoicing is the last thing you think of when bad things happen. It makes you wonder if prayer lit the candle of his heart in the eeriness of prison as surely as light provided sight for his eyes to scratch on papyrus his ink of grace, peace, and hope. Prayer next to the dung and prayer in the darkness when hope seems nonexistent remain as absolute necessities.

Never mind that Philippians, prayer, Lydia, and *rejoice* must have been on C. S. Lewis' mind when he wrote, "Joy is the serious business of

heaven."[2] Lewis reminds us that prayer awakens us, helps us take in the "patches of God-Light" as radiant as light breaking through the trees in a dark forest; and, since Jesus' model prayer known as the Lord's Prayer, and His prayer of agony in the Garden of Gethsemane serve as a way to pray in despair, prayer requires gut-wrenching honesty: "We must lay before Him what is in us, not what ought to be in us."[3] Everybody needs a dung gate; but before you get there you must first open the heart to prayer, to God, and—for all its worth—to the life of God in prayer.

I have not forgotten Paul and dung, nor Lydia and her prayers. Hang on. Lydia prayed to receive Christ down by the river, invited Paul and his companions to her villa in the hills, and helped start the first church in Europe, Lydia being one of its first converts. Not that Paul was finished sharing the Gospel.

On the way to a place of prayer (*proseuche*; verb form is *proseuchomai*, "to pray as a devotion"), Paul met a slave girl filled with an evil spirit, possessed of a soothsaying spirit like a

2 C. S. Lewis, *Letters to Malcolm Chiefly on Prayer* (New York: Harcourt, repr. 1992), 93.

3 Lewis, *Letters to Malcolm Chiefly on Prayer*, 91, 22.

modern-day tarot card reader in a tent who predicts the future by cards or by reading the lines on the palm of your hand. The fortune teller lady charged money for her bold predictions, but no one could predict whether anything she said actually came true, or if she just had insight into the human psyche, or human nature, human habits, or if she was a trickster like a magician pulling a rabbit out of a hat. No doubt her real magic was the money she counted at the end of the day. Apparently she filled her owner's coffers with piles of money, but she had an empty heart, or a troubled heart at best.

For some inexplicable reason, she followed Paul and his Christ-servants, including a man named Silas. The woman followed behind and shouted, "These men are servants of the Most High God, who are telling you the way to be saved" (Acts 16:17, NIV). The lady annoyed Paul for days, like a fly that needed to be swatted, or like bees building a hive over your front door. So one day as she followed, Paul whirled around, looked her in the eye, and shouted back to her, or more than likely the evil spirit. Paul yelled, "In the name of Jesus Christ I command you to come out of her!" At that moment the spirit left her" (Acts 16:18, NIV).

If troubled hearts need a wakeup call, a shout to empty the dung of the past, and a voice to set the future free from fortune-telling so the soul can fly on eagle's wings in a new direction toward God's good fortune, then Paul offered that voice "in Jesus's name." It never hurts to call on Jesus's name to rid the heart of past darkness and flood the heart with the Light of God's amazing grace. The spirit left her as simple as that. Sacred dung dumps evil in the Dung Gate and replaces it with grace no less. Sacred moments slip in, in a split second, in a shout, and in the surprise of sudden grace. All you have to do is open your ears, or your heart for that matter.

Bad things can give way to good things by God's grace.

However, the next thing we know, the good thing for the slave girl becomes a bad thing for Paul. Life, for all it's worth, is like walking on the edge of a precipice: Keep your feet firmly planted beneath you on the rock; enjoy the view; beware of strange winds that blow. But even in the bad things, Paul never loses sight of the good things; he keeps his feet firmly planted on the Rock, and waits for God's grace to shake things up.

From all we can tell, the slave girl's new-found grace incited her to take the sign out of the window and end her run at fortune-telling. Her fortune rested on the grace of Jesus now. Her shop owners, the ones to whom she paid the rent and shared her wealth from fortune-telling and collections of the clanketty-clank of Roman coins dropped into a bronze bowl, apparently appeared none too happy.

Luke records this admirably, descriptively, and accurately. I am no literary critic in the vein of Dr. Samuel Johnson, but Luke the physician has a way with words and this is one fine piece of narrative prose:

> *"When the owners of the slave girl realized that their hope of making money was gone, they seized Paul and Silas and dragged them into the marketplace to face the authorities. They brought them before the magistrates and said, 'These men are Jews, and are throwing our city into an uproar by advocating customs unlawful for us Romans to accept or practice.'*
>
> *The crowd joined in the attack against Paul and Silas, and the magistrates ordered*

them to be stripped and beaten. After they
had been severely flogged, they were thrown
into prison, and the jailer was commanded
to guard them carefully. Upon receiving such
orders, he put them in the inner cell and fas-
tened their feet in the stocks" (Acts 16:19-24,
NIV).

Faster than Paul could say "spirit come out
of her," Paul and his traveling evangelist Silas
were thrown in jail. In the agora or marketplace,
officials tossed Roman law in their faces; accused
them of upsetting the local economy; politicized
the event with a public display of Roman power,
protest, flogging; and threw them into prison.

What's interesting is that Paul himself writes
from prison, *phulake* in Greek, "a guarding," and
later in Old French what was known as a *donjon*,
"a hole, a forgotten place;" later archaically translated as *dungeon*, "a dark underground prison."
In medieval times the word described "a castle's
keep," a fortified tower. Translated in Saxon the
word translated, *dung*, an underground cellar,
and still again the word *dungeon*. It is thought the
word came to be associated with underground
chambers, torture chambers, and latrines, that is,
toilets. Paul landed in prison in Philippi in a dark

place, a *donjon*, an underground cellar, a place aligned with dung.

I promise you. I am not making this up. Research uncovers a lot of stuff. So what did Paul do in the dungeon among the dung? He sat there among other prisoners. He pondered his fate. He pondered God's grace. And then he and Silas began to sing. Midnight set in as Paul belted out songs in the shadows and songs in the night. Paul and Silas sang the special music of praise to God while their congregation of prisoners listened.

Then faster than Paul could say *Philippi*, the crackling and shaking of earth and rock in the dungeon joined the chorus of song. An earthquake split the jail and all dung broke loose. Violence rocked the foundations. Prison doors shook loose from their hinges and rattled loose. Chains busted. The clanketty-clank of chains awoke the prison keeper, the jailer in charge of Paul and Silas and the other prisoners. Things were shaken as were the prisoners and the jailer. Paul and Silas seemed unshaken.

Believing he had lost his prisoners with gates now open, the jailer, fearing Roman oppression and brutality much more than the earthquake, and much more than life itself, made a decision. He lifted his sword, a *machaira*, a short, single-blade knife or sword, from the sheath, ready to find a chink in the armor and end it all right there in the dungeon. Peter used the same type of sword (*machaira*) to cut off the high priest's servant's ear, Malchus, in the garden of Gethesemane. It's one thing to slice off an ear, very much another to aim at your own heart.

Paul singing, and one earthquake later now Paul shouting, he informs the jailer that all prisoners are accounted for. No one has escaped. The jailer asks what it takes to be saved, believes in Jesus, and revels in joy. The next thing you know, Paul is at the jailer's house, eating at his table, and baptizing his whole family. You have to admire the entire scene, the ministry, and Paul's evangelistic success or, better yet, the mysterious movement of God's Spirit all in a day's work.

You have to guess that Paul never lived a dull life, rarely approached boredom, and that life for him was one like a paratrooper jumping out of one airplane, parachuting, hitting land with both feet, and then racing to the airport to do it again.

Paul writes his letter to the Philippians, remembering prayer, a prayer garden, a slave girl's soul, and a hair-raising experience of jail, an earthquake, a wing and a prayer, and a meal at the house of the jailer in the banquet-feast of joy. Paul writes from Rome and remembers just like you remember your first date, your best friend in elementary school, or the smell of pie in your grandmother's house. Paul remembers the wild moments, the wind and the quake, and the wind of the spirit no less than by God's grace that changed sinners to saints and rearranged their priorities. He remembers and he writes a letter, a letter of love, of appreciation for their help, and as a reminder not to forget in the mundane drab of life to rejoice in Jesus. Rejoice! Again, I say, rejoice!

When Paul writes he uses that word again: dung. Paul thanks the Philippians, probably thinking of Lydia, a slave girl, and a jailer and his kids. He appreciates their good work as partners and God's good work still working. He celebrates how the chains of prison allowed him to speak in the dungeon about God's grace. Later, in another letter, Paul told Timothy, "Remember Jesus Christ, raised from the dead, descended from David. This is my gospel, for which I am suffering even to the point of being chained like a criminal. But God's word is not chained" (2 Timothy 2:8-10, NIV).

God's grace cannot be chained. I find, as Paul did, people need reminders of what they already know. Life works that way. Grace is not chained.

Paul's letter talked preachers, the good kind and the bad kind, of life in Christ, of Christ's humility on the cross, and how their faith should "shine like stars." The gospel by God's grace should do enough in you and mean enough to you that you eradicate the darkness, shine light in the crevices to scatter the evil roaches, and refresh both sinners and saints in their struggle for light and grace. Then Paul laments their trials and instructs them, "Watch out for those dogs" (Philippians 3:2).

Those dogs on Paul's quest in ink to write his friends in Philippi in remembrance, caused his own memory to jog in defense of who he was, where he had come from, what he had been, and under God's grace what God had made him. Paul's use of the words *those dogs* and what he writes after those words makes you think Paul himself had been one of them. Maybe he knew what it was to act like one of *those dogs*.

Those dogs, like Paul once, might have reason to boast in their fleshly and earthly accomplishments. Paul pulls out his curriculum vitae, his resume, and his up-to-date biographical sketch: "...though I myself have reasons for such confidence. If anyone else thinks he has reasons to put confidence in the flesh, I have more: circumcised on the eighth day, of the people of Israel, of the tribe of Benjamin, a Hebrew of Hebrews; in regard to the law, a Pharisee; as for zeal, persecuting the church; as for legalistic righteousness, faultless" (Philippians 3:4-6, NIV). Everybody needs a resume and everybody delivers their accomplishments in moments of defense as Paul did, or maybe in moments of explanation, as all of us do when we interview for a job.

It makes you wonder if Paul himself remembers these accomplishments and joined *those dogs* as a harsh critic of Christianity, a defender of Pharisaic Judaism, and running with a wild pack of teeth-snarling, voice-growling dogs. Makes you wonder if Paul had something specific in mind, something he had witnessed, watched first hand, and maybe even participated in. Was Paul consciously or unconsciously remembering himself as a dog the day Stephen was stoned and the participants placed their clothes at Paul's feet with him, not lifting so much as a finger, except maybe to smooth the clothes of the angry, rock-throwing Jewish nationalists (Acts 7:58-59). Maybe Stephen's use of the word *stiff-necked* in reference to the Pharisees was what got him in trouble as he defended the faith before the Sanhedrin. Maybe Paul's memory of the event made his past accomplishments seem small, or even dung-like in comparison to that awful day. Maybe Paul remembered his persecution of the church at Jerusalem, his barking and dragging people out of their homes in a fury of unholy fire, and his biting ferocity in throwing Christians in prison.

Paul majored in legalistic righteousness at one time and double-majored in running with the dogs; but, the more he remembered, the more he recognized either God's sense of humor or God's wit transferred to Paul or, more than likely, God's light, God's shock, and God's amazing grace. Be careful of barking back at your critics, enemies, and opponents lest one day you suddenly by God's grace show up on the other side, on their side, or like them, *those dogs.*

Paul remembers, then appears to want to forget. He writes:

> *"But whatever was to my profit I now consider loss for the sake of Christ. What is*

more, I consider everything a loss compared to the surpassing greatness of knowing Christ Jesus my Lord, for whose sake I have lost all things. I consider them rubbish [dung, skuba-lon], that I may gain Christ and be found in him, not having a righteousness of my own that comes from the law, but that which is through faith in Christ — the righteousness that comes from God and is by faith. I want to know Christ and the power of his resurrection and the fellowship of sharing in his suffer-ings, becoming like him in his death, and so, somehow, to attain to the resurrection from the dead. Not that I have already obtained all this, or have already been made perfect, but I press on to take hold of that for which Christ Jesus took hold of me. Brothers, I do not con-sider myself yet to have taken hold of it. But one thing I do: Forgetting what is behind and straining toward what is ahead, I press on to-ward the goal to win the prize for which God has called me heavenward in Christ Jesus" (Philippians 3:7-14, NIV).

Everybody needs a Dung Gate. Did you see that? Paul's past accomplishments, past

misery, and past embarrassments he considered dung. Apparently, metaphorically and spiritually, he walked to the Dung Gate, placed all his accomplishments, misery, past sin, and past hopelessness at the Dung Gate, and walked away from it. He placed the past at the Dung Gate, stood at the gate in a voice of praise to God, put his past behind, and began to press on to the mark of the high calling of God in Christ Jesus.

This is the way it goes: revelation yields to inspiration which births transformation. Paul remembers not to forget to remember that day on the Damascus Road when a light shone, the glory fell, grace moved in, and Christ made him a different person, a changed person, a new person. The revelation of Christ (I am Jesus!) imposed inspiration (Saul no more, but Paul) and gave way to transformation (Paul began to preach in the synagogues in Damascus that Jesus is the son of God! [Acts 9]. God's amazing grace might make you laugh or cause you to scratch your head in disbelief or amazement: One day you hold rocks and coats to persecute Christians, and another day in a flash of light you become one, cemented to the Rock and clothed in a new joy, a new righteousness, and a new grace.

And this is precisely what I think I have been trying to say. There will come a point in life when bad things happen, when sin sours the heart, or when life in its misery creates a dung heap in the heart and you will need to, by God's grace, carry it all to the Dung Gate, send it to the fire, start over, and press forward, even upward toward God's new calling, his high calling, and his grace calling.

You can no more live in the past than you can put a fallen leaf back on a tree or make a river run backward or turn a frog into a tadpole or, like a magician pulling a rabbit out of a hat, turn a monarch butterfly into a green caterpillar.

Reading Paul's use of dung in Philippians 3:8, and knowing his extensive knowledge of Judaism, the Old Testament Scriptures like the Torah, historical books, prophets, and poetry like the Psalms, and his personal journey through the actual terrain of Jerusalem make you also wonder if he was familiar with the term *dung heap*. If I were guessing, I would say he was familiar with the term. A dung heap combined with dirt and dung as a pile of manure. More will be said about this in the next chapter. But a dung heap might also indicate what you might find just beyond the Dung Gate in the ravines and disgusting valley below.

Who knows but maybe Philippi had a dung heap where the Philippians dumped their trash and refuse like the Jerusalemites dumped theirs beyond the Dung Gate? If all this seems a little confusing, just suffice it to say that every Monday I take out the trash and you have a trash day yourself like people in Philippi or Jerusalem, and on some days we need to dump our sin, our past, our misery, our hatred, our prejudice, our anger, our malice, our selfishness, our foolishness, and our bitterness into the dung heap beyond the Dung Gate like we would rotten tomatoes, coffee grounds, molded bread, dirty diapers, or sour milk. Maybe the Dung Gate is the place where you pile up a dung heap of confession of sin.

1 John 1:9 (NIV) says, "If we confess our sins, he is faithful and just and will forgive us our sins and purify us from all unrighteousness." Here we confess sins and aim by God's grace for a fresh start.

Maybe the Dung Gate represents a milestone like a historical marker as if to say, "I leave that behind. I enjoyed it or disliked it while it lasted. It's time to move forward. It's time to move ahead. It's time to tackle new adventures." You hang the marker as a reminder, either bad or good, and press forward, maybe with eagerness or hesitancy, maybe even with sadness or with the excitement of a woman jumping out of an airplane with a parachute for the first time. In the strength of God's grace you take the first step into your new adventure, life, or path. By hanging a historical marker you remember the past; appreciate it; learn from it; and, quite possibly, hope you never have to walk through anything like that again.

Or maybe the Dung Gate marks the spot or draws the line where you simply clean up some stuff in your life like spring cleaning. In an upsize world you downsize, or in your cluttered world you simplify, or in the chaos you make room for peace. You carry the stuff, the cluttered piles, and the chaos to the Dung Gate, dump the whole load and shout, "Be gone!" This cleansing experience symbolizes for you a fresh journey and a new commitment.

Spring cleaning of life and soul must be repeated occasionally for life to find balance, make sense, anchor your faith, and renew the weariness of life. Spiritual writer Kathleen Norris speaks of Christ's indwelling, how we sometimes need to *care* again, and how important faith remains in daily life. She says, "In our life of faith, then, as well as in our most intimate relationships with other people, our task is to transform the high romance of conversion, the fervor of religious call, into daily commitment."[4] You put the past in your rearview mirror, open your heart to God's wonderful surprise, and reach forward by His grace as you journey onward. New commitments spell new goals, new dreams, and necessitate the unfear of taking risks.

Or maybe you would describe what you need as *a change* or to change or to make some changes or to change as in making progress in life. The Dung Gate supplies the appropriate place in time to clean out the old, the past, or even some good from the past, dump it at the gate, and step away from the gate toward the better, best, and beyond the dung that makes you feel like a car stuck in the mud. C. S. Lewis reminds us, "Progress means not just changing, but changing for the better."[5] We change and venture from the past into the future. A bold step, a clear choice, and a forward movement requires an inspired change toward

4 Kathleen Norris, *The Quotidian Mysteries: Laundry, Liturgy and "Women's Work,"* (New York: Paulist Press, 1998), 78.

5 C.S. Lewis, *The Case for Christianity* (New York: Touchstone, 1996), 11.

progress, for the better, and toward personal renewal, an unfulfilled dream, or garden-fresh motivation. God provides the gate, but you have to provide the motivation. No one can make the change for you.

Back to the Dung Gate. When Nehemiah and the workers completed construction of the walls, a strange event then took place. Priests and Levites purified themselves ceremonially. Next they purified the people and then purified the walls and the gates. After this, two choirs formed, from all we can tell, near the Dung Gate. Nehemiah asked the leaders of Judah to climb to the top of the wall. Next, the two choirs proceeded, one choir in one direction toward the Dung Gate and the other in the opposite direction, apparently on the wall, walking and giving thanks. Nehemiah followed them until they made way on the walls, stopped at the Gate of the Guard, and eventually made their way to the house of God, the temple (Nehemiah 12:27-42).

Imagine the music, the singing, the instruments playing, and the spirit of joy. Imagine the leaders of Judah like Olympic athletes on a balance beam gingerly walking the wall in wild rejoicing in the overcoming spirit of past's remorse.

Imagine the leaders free on the wall, enjoying the scenery, and reveling in the joy of accomplishment and the overflow of God's grace.

Nehemiah pens the experience in his own words, "And on that day they offered great sacrifices, rejoicing because God had given them great joy. The women and children also rejoiced. The sound of rejoicing in Jerusalem could be heard far away" (Nehemiah 12:43, NIV). Did you see that? Thanksgiving and praise entered heaven's ears within earshot of the Dung Gate. Did you see that? Rejoicing came after hardship, after the trial and travail of construction, after the meanness of enemies, and after the past struggle for freedom and rebuilding the wall. Did you see that? Worship resulted in the aftermath of the hard work on the walls.

Is this any different than Paul and Silas singing in prison, their dungeon? Is this any different than Paul writing a letter to the Philippians in his own pit, in a Roman dungeon, and in a legal ordeal in Rome and exhorting them, "Rejoice in the Lord always. I will say it again: Rejoice!" (Philippians 4:4, NIV)? Is this any different than you standing on the wall near your Dung Gate after you dumped the past to move toward the future and declaring in a song of praise words of rejoicing to the Lord? Did you see that? Rejoicing after repentance, after rebuilding, or after renewal, serves as a requirement?

We rise on the wall, look to the heavens, give thanks to the Almighty, and sing out with powerful words like those of the mystic poet Gerard Manley Hopkins in *Pied Beauty*, "Glory be to God for dappled things!"[6] Of course, *dappled things* means the shaded areas, the lighter colored spots like those on a horse, the stains of the past if you will, or the splashed spots riddled with tears of hopelessness in days past now fully surrendered to the past and taken up in present songs of thanksgiving in the sunlight of fresh hope. And the hope is Christ.

You have this deep sense with both Nehemiah and Paul that God gets the last word, that the last word shines brighter than the ones before, and that standing on the wall near the Dung Gate with a song of rejoicing in your heart and on your lips sure beats sitting in a dung heap of past sins, miseries, and hopeless dung for that matter.

---

6 See Ryan, Thomas, Hopkins: *The Mystic Poets Series* (Woodstock, Vermont: SkyLight Paths Publishing, 2004), 59.

You can step into dung, it can stack up like trash, can fall into your life, and cause you to arrive at a place where you're stuck in the mud, but the good news remains: you do not have to live in the dung forever. By God's renewing grace you can carry it to the Dung Gate, dump it, catch one last whiff of the stench in the wind, climb the wall near the gate, thank God, and move on.

Everybody needs a Dung Gate because sometime in your life you will need a place, a time, and a moment to release the dung of the past so that you can move forward into the dynamite of the future. When you do this you discover afresh God's mercy and grace and Jesus our high priest, who, in a sense, has passed before us and passed through the heavens on our behalf. "Therefore, since we have a great high priest who has gone through the heavens, Jesus the Son of God, let us hold firmly to the faith we profess. For we do not have a high priest who is unable to sympathize with our weaknesses, but we have one who has been tempted in every way, just as we are — yet was without sin. Let us then approach the throne of grace with confidence, so that we may receive mercy and find grace to help us in our time of need" (Hebrews 4:14-16, NIV).

Nehemiah and Paul knew the importance of a Dung Gate as well as the joy of God's mercy and grace. They both knew, in God's unending mercy, they did not travel life alone because God went with each of them. They both knew of God's all-surpassing grace because God met their needs, provided a way out of the dung, and provided a way to clean up their lives with the freshest of scents.

Nehemiah wrote it down: "But in your great mercy you did not put an end to them or abandon them, for you are a gracious and merciful God" (Nehemiah 9:31, NIV). Paul wrote it down in the splash of sun rays painting the shadows in his prison cell: "But he [God] said to me, 'My grace is sufficient for you, for my power is made perfect in weakness.' Therefore I will boast all the more gladly about my weaknesses, so that Christ's power may rest on me. That is why, for Christ's sake, I delight in weaknesses, in insults, in hardships, in persecutions, in difficulties. For when I am weak, then I am strong" (2 Corinthians 12:9-10, NIV). Write this down: bad things happen. They really do. Good things happen, too. Grace happens, too. It all starts with a trip to the trash can, a trip to dump the past, a trip to the Dung Gate.

Still, all told, how strange that the Dung Gate also becomes a place of thanksgiving, of rejoicing, and of praise. When God makes you whole again, when you feel healthy again, when the spirit rises in the heart like the leaders of Judah on the walls, God's grace gives you the strength to carry on and the power to live life anew. And that's how it works: the dung piles up, the dung goes out, God's mercy and grace in thanksgiving move in, mercy takes over, and God's grace strengthens and freshens up heart and soul, life and limb. Suddenly, tears surrender to joy. You feel alive again. Joy returns. You can smile again.

Notes to the Reader

Oh dear reader, what do you think? Do you have a Dung Gate? Do you need one? Do you need one now? Have you thought about some junk you need to carry to the gate? Do you need a wheelbarrow to carry past sin, anger, hurt, bitterness, and/or mistakes?

Did you like my *wheelbarrow* image? I used it because spring arrives here in Texas as I write. Bluebonnets, orange Texas paintbrushes, and other wild flowers have sprouted beside roadsides, along highways, in fields, beside rivers and ponds, in ravines, and are cascading up narrow hills. Today the sun shines partly through the clouds. The wind blows. The bluebonnets on roadsides blow in the wind in a neat flowing arrangement like dominoes lined up and falling in perfect form and symmetry. God paints the Texas canvas a dazzling array of colors and adds sparkle in springtime.

By the way, I have really been thinking about this. If you do not have a Dung Gate, a place and time to dump the dung, the junk you step into, the refuse that falls on you, or the stuff that gets you stuck, your life is done in the dung. How many times have I seen people drowning in the dung? How many times have I watched people wallow and wail in the dung as if they were immature children playing in the mud and making mud pies? How many times have I observed people stuck in the dung and the dung stuck to them as if they cannot shake their feet free? If you do not dump the dung, you're done. Your life is over. Kiss life goodbye. Turn out the lights. The party's over!

By that I do not mean you have stopped breathing or you cannot go to work in the morning or pay your bills online or watch a baseball game on television or do the laundry or wash the

dishes or mow the lawn. I mean the quality of your life is diminished; you cease to live a life fully alive in God's dappled glory. How much better to be done with dung and get on with your life and the life God intended! The Dung Gate in your life serves as an exit from the past and an entrance into God's future promise and hope (Jeremiah 29:11).

When I finished this chapter, I stood up from my computer, shelved two books, one by C. S. Lewis and one by Kathleen Norris, and noticed a book on the shelf by Ryszard Kapuściński titled Travels with Herodotus. An author, bard, poet, and Greek historian, Herodotus, as best we can theorize, lived roughly from 484-420 B.C. Herodotus also traveled much of the known world at the time, wrote about the Persian wars between Greeks and non-Greeks, and described the geography of places and cities.

Herodotus tells how the invaders known as the fish-eaters from Persia compared their diets to those of the Ethiopians. The Ethiopians tended to live longer, albeit roughly one hundred and twenty years, on a diet of food like boiled meat and milk. The Persians lived approximately eighty years like one of their kings who had a diet of wheat-based bread and other food staples. Herodotus quotes an Ethiopian, "It was no wonder that their lives were so short, if they ate dung."[7] Herodotus uses the Greek word kopron, a reference to grain produced by manure spread among the dirt and seeds. Jesus used a form of this word in Luke 14:35 as an analogy for fertilizer. In the next chapter, I will explore dung as fertilizer in your life.

Ryszard Kapuściński records the second law of Herodotus in his travel pertaining both to human life and history, "Human happiness never remains long in the same place."[8] Herodotus and Ryszard Kapuściński remind us of the importance of memory, the struggle we all face on our journeys, and the quest to find justice amid injustice, peace amid the chaos, grace amid un-grace, and the light of happiness amid the darkness of so much unhappiness.

Herodotus, the father of history, I then confused with Heraclitus (lived around 500 B.C.), a Greek philosopher from Ephesus who felt most people sleep through life like Rip Van Winkle

---

7 Herodotus, *Histories III*, 22.

8 Ryszard Kapuściński, *Travels With Herodotus* (trans. By Klara Glowczewska; New York: Alfred A. Knopf, 2007), 85.

without any depth of understanding about the world, themselves, or life. Heraclitus said, "No man ever steps in the same river twice, for it's not the same river and he's not the same man." Known as the weeping philosopher who always wore dark clothing, he meant that a river constantly flows and you cannot step into the same river twice. What he did not say is equally true, "You can step into the same dung twice." For the record, that's why you need to get rid of it at the Dung Gate.

While I was writing this chapter, the whole concept of dung, the Dung Gate, and evil must have overwhelmed me. Yes, you can step into dung, it can stack up like trash, it can fall into your life like bird droppings and can cause you to arrive at a place where you're stuck in the mud. Jesus associated the Dung Gate and certain activities as a place of refuse, a place to cast evil things once and for all, and a place reserved for the separation of the holy and unholy.

Anyway, while writing this chapter or, more likely, after writing part of this chapter, I felt so overwhelmed by the thought of evil, final judgment, and the Dung Gate that I dreamed a bizarre dream. A black, red, and yellow snake made its way into my home in the upstairs hall. Was it a Texas coral snake, poisonous, associated with the family of snakes that includes cobras? I killed the snake, fell asleep upstairs on the carpet near the dead snake in the dream, only to awaken as the resurrected snake fell over the upstairs railing, slithered on the brown tile below and in front of the front door, then into the dining room where the table and all furniture for some strange reason had been removed. The dark brown cut wood on the dining room floor contrasted with the black, red, and yellow snake that now appeared larger than the snake that was dead upstairs. This dream happened near 6 a.m. one spring morning.

Startled, anxious, and suddenly alert, I woke up just as the snake birthed numerous baby snakes that began to race and wiggle through the house. Imagine hundreds of fast-moving baby snakes slithering and glistening as the light reflected off their skins and moving toward you! The dream was so vivid, I woke up, walked into the kitchen, turned on the lights, looked down the hall into the dining room, and saw no snakes.

Let me interpret the dream. Beware lest evil, once you think it has been destroyed, resurrects, multiplies before you can get your hands around it. Oh, I cannot say with confidence that the dream might actually mean that, but I can tell you my subconscious combined a news story I heard before I went to bed ("It's spring. Watch out for snakes. They're starting to move.") and my own words on *Gehenna* as evil (remember this I wrote earlier? "If all this sounds scary and even as you read the stench of black smoke and burnt toast in the toaster affects your mind and causes you to imagine *Gehenna* as a bad place, an evil place, a fiery place, and a dumping ground, it is"). Snakes, evil, and Gehenna mixed in my brain like witches brew, and the next thing you know my mind takes flight on a broom and I have a bad, nightmarish dream.

Take evil to the Dung Gate. Dump it there. Leave it there. I might even recommend going to sleep with good thoughts, the good news, the Bible in your brain, or a Dr. Seuss book dancing in your head before you retire to bed. Did you catch that? Head rhymes with bed. I like a good Dr. Seuss book. I love books. I love the Bible. Read a Psalm and fall sleep.

Oh, I almost forgot to tell you. Not long ago in Cambridge I made this discovery, as exciting as miners unearthing the gold in Philippi. I walked from the Tyndale House Biblical Research Center in Cambridge after a long morning of poring over the Greek word *ofeilo*, translated into English as *obligation*. On the way to get something to eat, right in front of King's College on the part of the street known as King's Parade, I took a right turn down an alleyway to a hole-in-the-wall bookshop. Inside the shop on shelves you will find crammed copies of the classics, poetry, history, theology, old maps, collections, used books purchased from professors' libraries, and old, notable, unique books. The bookshop sells new books; but, if you walk to the back of the store and turn left, presto, you find yourself in the room of wall-to-wall collections and rare books.

You probably do not want to know this, but I once found a rare two-volume set of books about Roman Law. While working on my Ph. D., I found myself stuck until I found a first edition copy of the prized book: Francis De Zulueta, *The Institutes of Gaius: Part I and II Text with Critical Notes and Translation.* Clarendon Press published the book in 1946. I paid the small sum of twenty-five British pounds for both volumes and before that day ended I was unstuck, on my way to writing again, and feeling like I had just been handed free tickets to

Downton Abbey or the Dallas Maverick game or like a kid in a candy store. For the record, I do not watch Downton Abbey regularly but would like to see the place; I always welcome free tickets to the Mavs game; and I do not eat that much candy. But if I did, maybe I would not have bizarre dreams about colorful snakes.

Oh, I am telling you about a book I found. Yes, I did find Francis De Zulueta's two- volume set; but on the day I am writing about, I also found a 1943 edition of *A Preface to Paradise Lost* by C.S. Lewis. Can you believe it, a 1943 edition? A rare book? A gold mine? I grabbed the book, flipped through its pages, bought the book for twenty British pounds, and walked back toward the street. Later that day I lumbered down to Magdalen College in Cambridge where Lewis taught, stood in the entrance doorway, and imagined him walking through the door wearing a hat, his tweed coat, and holding a handful of shuffled papers to grade.

The book begins by discussing Epic poetry. The word *epic* appears misused today. I heard a woman say, "It was an epic fail;; a man says of a basketball play, "It was an epic dunk;" a young person who saw a movie, "Epic!" The word *epic* usually refers to narrative poetry, rare storied poetry that details a change in the course of history like Homer's *Iliad* about Greece or Beowulf in England. Lewis describes certain features of epic poetry in the book. I started reading the book while writing this book. Lo and behold, Lewis discusses on page 19 *oral techniques* used in epic poetry and "stockwords, phrases, or even whole lines."[9] Stock words or phrases indicate a repetitive line. Good writing, oral poetry, and epic words find rhythm, repetition, and rehearse a theme so as to cause the hearer to like what is being read, remember it, and be moved by it.

What Lewis describes as a technique, I liken to the technical aspects of writing which lead me to tell you how *A Preface to Paradise Lost* helped me in writing this book. My *stock expression* in this chapter is "everybody needs a Dung Gate," a place to dump the past, to confess past sin, and a place to stand and declare a word of praise to God while acknowledging both without and within, "This is behind me. I am moving forward by God's grace." So as the old song in the Disney movie *Frozen* allures us, "Let it go!" C. S. Lewis once quipped

---

9 C. S. Lewis, *A Preface to Paradise Lost* (London: Oxford University Press, 1943), 19.

that "praise almost seems to be inner health made audible."[10]

When we dump the past at the Dung Gate, we can stand in God's grace and by His freedom on the wall, and declare His praise. Inner health, inner cleansing, and inner catharsis set the soul free to fly on eagle's wings. A word of praise to the God of grace serves the order of the day. Praise becomes your personal *stock phrase* and your repetitive soul praise of thanksgiving to God for his grace poured out on you.

Oh, and while I almost finished writing this chapter I turned on the radio and listened to music while I shaved. The Russian writer Vladimir Nabokov (1899-1977) spent three years studying modern languages at the esteemed Trinity College in Cambridge. Nabokov said, "I don't think that an artist should bother about his audience. His best audience is the person he sees shaving in the morning." Nabokov was a genius. He might have been crazy. The Greeks called genius "a little spirit," *daimononion*, or divine fury. Maybe the fortune-telling slave girl in Philippi had a demon or *daimononion*, or un-divine fury, that is, until Jesus

---

10 C.S. Lewis, *Reflections on the Psalms* (London: Harcourt Brace & Company, 1958), 94.

cleared out the dung and delivered her past to the Dung Gate. When I shave in the morning I think deep thoughts about hurling comets, worldwide political debates, about the deep hurt in our world, and deep theological thoughts about God's compassion and His wondrous love and grace.

Nabokov despised academic mediocrities. He more than likely despised the fact that many academics rejected him. He loved lepidoptery, that is, *butterflies*. I love butterflies. He wrote a book titled *The Real Life of Sebastian Knight*, a novel that might suggest that our lives are like knights, moved and played on a board like a game of chess. "Is one's life one's own," Oxford scholar John Sutherland surmises in analyzing Nabokov's book. "An artist should destroy manuscripts after publication…," Nabokov once insisted. Maybe I should destroy my Sacred Dung manuscript before publication.[11]

By the way, your life is not your own, according to the Apostle Paul in 1 Corinthians. "Do you not know that your body is a temple of the Holy Spirit, who is in you, whom you have received

---

11 Adapted and quoted from John Sutherland, *Lives of the Novelists: A History in Fiction in 294 Lives* (New Haven: Yale University Press, 2012), 412-415.

from God? You are not your own; you were bought at a price. Therefore honor God with your body" (1 Corinthians 6:19-20, NIV). He later wrote, "But by the grace of God I am what I am, and his grace to me was not without effect. No, I worked harder than all of them — yet not I, but the grace of God that was with me" (1 Corinthians 15:10, NIV).

What I'm saying to you, beloved, is that if God's grace slew Paul's past, He can do the same for you. You are what you are by God's grace. I am what I am by God's grace. Enjoy His grace. And, when bad things happen, surrender it all to God's amazing grace.

No, I have not forgotten about the music I heard while I shaved. I offer my sincerest apologies for the Nabokov digression. I am not sure where that came from. When I shaved I heard a song by worship leader Kari Jobe on the radio. Like epic poetry or a repetitive phrase or stock words, Kari Jobe sang *I Am Not Alone* with those memorable, repeated words: "I am not alone." If you find your-self in deep water, in the fire, in a storm, or in the dung for that matter, by God's grace, you are not alone if you trust Christ. Trust Christ, climb the wall, stand on the wall and give thanksgiving and praise to God for that! You are not alone!

So here is spring, and God paints Texas bluebonnets blue and His glory dazzles and dapples.
In Houston, public officials debate whether or
not to tear down the USA's first Roman coliseum,
the historic and—at this stage, nostalgic—Astrodome. When Mickey Mantle of the New York Yankees hit the first home run in the indoor Astrodome, people celebrated the feat and the august
structure of human ingenuity. Today, fifty years
later, the Astrodome sits dwarfed by an NFL football stadium, now nothing more than an old, de-
caying structure piled with junk and dung like an
old, trashed barn on the old family farm.

Historically and nostalgically, like most of
us in life, people want to hang on to the past. But
sometimes it's best to let it go, level the past, and
move forward. Herodotus reminds us we can remember it and savor it, but not dwell on it too
much. Heraclitus signals to the brain to remember, life like a river keeps moving, and we need
to keep moving, too. Nehemiah calls for a Dung
Gate, a place for refuse, but also a sacred place to
thank God in spirit and to sing praise to God for
his past blessings and past/present/future glory.
The Apostle Paul acknowledges, "What is more,
I consider everything a loss compared to the

surpassing greatness of knowing Christ Jesus my Lord, for whose sake I have lost all things. I consider them rubbish [dung, *skubalon*], that I may gain Christ" (Philippians 3:8, NIV).

I do not know about the Astrodome, but officials might have to level it, blow it up, and explode it with dynamite so they can build a new structure. And this is precisely what Paul adds after his dung comment, "I want to know Christ and the power of his resurrection and the fellowship of sharing in his sufferings, becoming like him... (Philippians 3:10, NIV). Becoming like Christ and knowing Him in His power (literally, dynamite, *dunamis* in Greek), means you will have to dynamite the dung, level the past, and allow God in his power to start and work his new in you.

All told, I'll say it again: If you do not get rid of the dung, you're done. But start with God's power and his grace, and the dung becomes fertilizer for tomorrow's fruit. Let's call that grace, sacred refuse, a place to start fresh again. Everybody needs a second chance.

Write this down: Everybody needs a Dung Gate. Everybody needs a dung gate to dump the past and renew the sacred grace of God's future in you. Sacred refuse paves the way for new vistas.

Now turn the page and move from sacred refuse to sacred refrain. Investigate with me dung as fertilizer to soften the soul for future days.

Sacred Refrain

From Loss to Gain

*"The grower of trees, the gardener, the man born
to farming,*

whose hands reach into the ground and sprout,

to him soil is a divine drug. He enters into death

*yearly, and comes back rejoicing. He has seen the
light lie down*

in the dung heap, and rise again in the corn.

His thought passes along the row ends like a mole.

What miraculous seed has he swallowed

that the unending sentence of his love flows out of
his mouth

like a vine clinging in the sunlight, and like water

descending in the dark?"

~Wendell Berry, a poem, "Man Born to Farming"[12]

Write this down: One day you will wake up in the dark wilderness and it will be just what the doctor ordered.

Back in the day when life thrived as roses minus the thorns, and life glowed in simple sunrises and sunsets, I attended seminary. I graduated, but not without first having to pass Systematic Theology. The class met at 8 am, and by mid-term only eight students remained in the class. The professor of Systematic Theology possessed a name exactly like the tutor C. S. Lewis had as a young man: Dr. Kirkpatrick. C. S. Lewis studied under Kirkpatrick at The Great Bookham in Surrey in 1918 in preparation for entrance exams at Oxford, England. I studied under Dr. Kirkpatrick in a Fort Worth Baptist seminary in preparation for survival of the fittest in the land of ministry and church.

---

12 Wendell Berry, *Collected Poems: 1957-1982* (New York: North Point Press, 1987), 103

C. S. Lewis called the professor *Knock* in his letters to his brother and his father and at other times *The Great Knock*. Lewis recalled visiting *Knock* one day after the erudite Greek-Latin-philosopher-logic professor had been in the hospital. Lewis described *Knock* as an old man "there among the cabbages, in his shirt and wearing 'Sunday' trousers, still digging and smoking his villainous pipe."[13] Lewis appreciated the reminiscences, noticed *Knock* fussing at the maid, and yet remarked in their discussions "how often my opinions were shown to be based ('bazed' as the sage pronounced it) on an insufficient knowledge of the subject!"[14] You get the impression that *Knock* knocked Lewis down a few notches; taught him how to analyze, think, and write; and challenged him like no other teacher.

My *Great Knock* in Fort Worth proved to be Dr. Kirkpatrick of my seminary experience. He used a book bigger than an old unabridged dictionary entitled *The Foundations of Dogmatics* by the German theologian Otto Weber. Weber is pronounced with a "v," as in *Veber*. All the great

---

13 C. S. Lewis, *Letters of C. S. Lewis* (New York: Harcourt, 1988), 82.

14 Lewis, *Letters of C. S. Lewis*, 82.

knock theologians possess German names often mispronounced. I had no idea about dogmatics, systematic theology, Christology, or any of those other *ology* words. I had little knowledge of theologians like Calvin, Schleiermacher, Niebuhr, Pelagius, Pannenberg, Anselm, Arius, Arminius, Augustine, or Bultmann, Origen, or Karl Barth. I mispronounced *Barth* with a "th" sound like tooth and felt the ire of the Great Knock. I learned theology, survived *Knock*, the sleepy-eyed class, and the final exam.

One day the Great Knock started reflecting about the church. His eyes began to water, and he looked misty-eyed. He spoke of his love for the church and Christ, albeit ecclesiology and Christology. Had he been hurt by the church and felt the pain of it in lecturing? Had nostalgia like standing over your grandmother's grave risen up in his soul and spilled misty tears? Had love for the church warmed his heart and renewed his soul like dew on the morning grass?

Not long after that tearful reflection, he waxed eloquent on a theological sermon. A sermon departed from his norm of flashy theological words and eschatological ponderances of Scripture, Christian deep thinking, and philosophical meanderings like his favorite Pannenberg, process theology, salvation history, and a theology of hope. His wax-eloquent sermon felt like the rhythm of an old-style hell-fire-and-brimstone sermon in a country church.

"One day you're going to go through a wilderness experience. One day. Everybody in the ministry goes through a wilderness experience. Everybody needs a wilderness experience," he preached in his own words, "a kerygmatic message," that is, a message from the Greek *kerygma* that is translated as *preaching*.

He smiled as he looked through his Bonhoeffer-like wire-rimmed spectacles. He peered and then stared at the ceiling as if looking into heaven itself as the light radiated beneath the fluorescents. Since that day, I forgot some theology, learned to think theologically, resisted systems of theology, and concluded we're all in need of Christ's salvation and love in our own hearts, and that most of the people I knew including me struggled and drew every breath in the theology of hope. Hope anchored us in storms and kept the sails filled with air to move us forward on windy days and calm days in the sea of life.

Then it happened. I pastored two churches that seemed like a sunset cruise in the Bahamas. Smooth sailing became the mantra, until one day, I must have hit a sand bar because the sailboat hit rock bottom and the storm ripped the sails to boot. I had showed up in a church looking for the sunset cruise of the beautiful Bahamas; yet found myself shipwrecked on the island of Malta, afraid, uncertain about my future, and trying to fend off venomous snakes.

At age twenty-six I delivered the good news, offered *kerygma* as soul food in preaching, scattered seeds of God's love, and watched the church decline from 140 people to less than one hundred. After I stayed at that church for twenty years, I later recalled those hard, harsh wilderness days by saying, "When I first came I took the church from 140 to 100...and it only took six weeks. Then God took it from there." The church grew to more than a thousand in the next twenty years, but who could forget the Sunday all my child-care workers quit on me, yes all, or crying in the church parking lot one cold February night at my failures, and the only major industry laying off 1500 workers a month at a local nuclear plant during my first year.

One day you're going to go through a wilderness experience. One day. Everybody in the ministry goes through a wilderness experience. Everybody needs wilderness experience."

Did I tell you to write this down? One day you will wake up in the dark wilderness and it will be just what the doctor ordered. In the wilderness I learned to trust God, pray with guts, study the Scriptures, and love people, even the unlovable enemies who like snakes aimed to poison my soul. The storm raged and calmed down. The rain stopped after the storm. A drought ensued. I woke up in the wilderness with a wild coyote here and there and some cacti and barely enough drinking water to stay alive.

As time marched, I learned a theology of hope. The church began to grow by God's grace, and I survived to enjoy God, His grace, His people, and the intricacies and challenges of ministry. Like Abraham in the Old Testament I learned that against all hope I could hope and believe the Gospel (Romans 4:18). Like Jacob I recognized in my wrestling match with God, the church, and myself that I could by faith look "forward to the city with foundations, whose architect and builder is God" (Hebrews 11:10, NIV). Like Joseph reconciling with his brothers I learned the value of recounting God's simple blessings, of hope in famine, of hope in the shadows of life's lean days, and of hope in the anxiety, angst, and forgiveness of God's love by His grace. Like Moses I valued the journey from exile by exodus to the wilderness to the land of promise.

And so let's return to the subject of the wilderness, your wilderness experience, and the dung of the wilderness.

One day it occurred to me that all the people God used entered at one time in their lives into a wilderness experience. Abraham exiled from Nahor on an unknown wilderness journey until he arrived in God's land. Jacob wrestled with God in an existential crisis of faith in grace, personal agony, and belief before God changed his name from Jacob, *supplanter, cheater, trickster*, to Israel, *Prince of God*. Only the existential wilderness of God's grace transforms you from a trickster to a prince.

David spent many days on the run, in caves, and in the turmoil of loneliness and wilderness. Later the wilderness experiences, the grief, loneliness, and pain of the hard, harsh, wilderness experiences inspired him to write the psalms. God's grace can turn bad things into good things.

The prophets from Isaiah to Jeremiah to Amos to Malachi to John the Baptist each in his own right survived the wilderness and its harshness.

Fast forward to the Apostle Paul writing about dung to the Philippians. A quick study of his life finds three years where we know virtually nothing about his pilgrimage. We do know about Paul's conversion from Judaism to Christianity, from law to grace, from the shadow of the good things to come under the laws of Moses to the light of the better way under the wisdom of Jesus (Hebrews 10:1-25). Once a persecutor of the church on the road to Damascus, Paul encounters Christ's flash of light from heaven. Paul uses the Greek word *periastrapto*, a word that Galen, the physician of the Roman court and emperor (A.D. 129-199) who wrote *Method of Medicine*,[15] used to speak of the opacity of a wound to the eye. In other words, the bright flash of light like lightning caused a wound to the eye that resulted in cloudiness, dimness, even darkness. Paul's educated choice of words appears interesting because the

---

15 Galen, *Method of Medicine* V.9-13.

light caused temporary darkness, a kind of wilderness if you are used to seeing.

The men traveling with Paul only heard a thunderous sound, the sound of a voice from all I can tell, did not see a person much less a thing, yet saw the stumbling, fumbling Paul shot like a dead man to the ground. I imagine he stammered and stuttered and fluttered, feeling his way around on the ground while trying to see. For three days Paul was blind and did not eat or drink anything in Damascus. Paul heard Jesus' voice; felt the weight of salvation's heart-stopping, heart-wrenching, heart-changing flash of life-change, and asked, "Who are you, Lord?" (Acts 9:5, NIV). The severity and the humor of the moment strikes me: "Who are you, Lord" as if he already knew that his enemy had come to collect the rent due, to ransack his camp, and take the spoils besides. In the flash of light and in the black of darkness Jesus replied, "I am Jesus, whom you are persecuting…. Now get up and go into the city, and you will be told what you must do" (Acts 9:5-6, NIV).

All at once, Paul's once-upon-a-time enemy became Paul's friend, and grace began to drip into his heart like medicine fed intravenously in the arm at the hospital or, better yet, like honey dripping into your soul from the honeycomb or, even still, like misty-eyed rain dripping drops of joy into the mind after a drought. Grace has a way of finding us if only we open our eyes. And grace has a way of stopping the bad road we're on to lead us down a new road. Grace also has a way of wounding us so that we can become healers for others by God's grace in future days. I will say more about this in the next chapter.

Paul experienced salvation, God's light, and God's joy in a flash on the road. Listen to him describe what happens next: "For you have heard of my previous way of life in Judaism, how intensely I persecuted the church of God and tried to destroy it. I was advancing in Judaism beyond many Jews of my own age and was extremely zealous for the traditions of my fathers. But when God, who set me apart from birth and called me by his grace, was pleased to reveal his Son in me so that I might preach him among the Gentiles, I did not consult any man, nor did I go up to Jerusalem to see those who were apostles before I was, but I went immediately into Arabia and later returned to Damascus. Then after three years, I went up to Jerusalem to get acquainted with Peter and stayed with him fifteen days. I saw none of the other apostles

— only James, the Lord's brother. I assure you before God that what I am writing you is no lie" (Gal 1:13-20, NIV).

Did you see what Paul said? Not the part about the "what I am writing you is no lie," but the part about Arabia, three years, and then he went to Jerusalem. Paul's wilderness experience might be summed up in three phases: the short-lived blindness for three days, the acceptance by Christ but initial rejection by the disciples, and his three-year exile to Arabia. The blindness came as a pause to arrest his senses, his heart and soul. The rejection came as a sign to trust God first, not man. The trip to Arabia came as preparation for future ministry.

If I sound like I speak with confidence on such matters, I do. Each of us in life needs a sacred moment when we rest, reflect, digest, drink down deep, and take in what God does in us. Each of us will face temporary rejection, even betrayal at the hands of Judas to remind us to trust in the Lord alone. Each of us will have a period or periods in our Christian lives where a wilderness becomes a dry period, or a place of exile where God actually stops the action and ministry to prepare us for future action and ministry.

We know nothing, absolutely nothing of Paul's trek to Arabia. Bible scholars speculate he stayed near Damascus. Others guess that he went to Mount Sinai, the so-called *wilderness of Sinai*, the place where God met Moses on the Mount and revealed his word, *The Ten Words*, the Ten Commandments. What ever happened in Arabia, two things remain true: First, Paul's wilderness experience solidified his faith in God as well as his theology of belief in the person and work of Jesus the Christ. Second, what happened there in the beginning of his immature faith strengthened and prepared him in maturity toward a more mature faith ready to defend, minister, and preach the Gospel in the power of the cross. Apparently, a bad thing, the wilderness, paves the way for the good things to come, God's grace, preaching, church, ministry, and Paul's letters.

The timeless Biblical scholar J. B. Lightfoot summarizes Paul's wilderness journey to Arabia, "It is a mysterious pause, a moment of suspense in the Apostle's history, a breathless calm which ushers in the tumultuous storm of his active missionary life."[16] The wilderness swirled with sus-

---

16 J. B. Lightfoot, *The Epistle of Saint Paul to the Galatians* (2nd ed.; Grand Rapids: Zondervan, 1957), 87.

pense. Immediately after conversion Paul went to the house of a man named Judas, a common name. Ananias, a Christian, received a vision to go to that house and find the man of Tarsus praying. He went and found Paul, prayed for him as the scales fell off Paul's eyes. Paul's blindness vanished and he could see again. Paul was baptized, regained strength, and began to preach in the synagogue in Damascus (Acts 9:10-25).

The suspense continued as the governor under King Aretas IV wanted Paul arrested as a plot to take his life unfolded. Paul knew of this plot and Christians let him down a wall in Damascus by ropes, and Paul escaped. His wilderness experience began with heart-pounding drama and gut-wrenching survival. That was hardly a glamorous way to begin a faith-journey with Christ.

Let's return to Lightfoot's mysterious pause. If you look back at the people God used, you'll notice a mysterious pause, a waiting period, or what I describe as a wilderness experience happens at some point in their lives. *Mysterious* advances the sense of God's Spirit at work in secret and also creates the suspense of "God, what will you do next?" It might generate a pouring out of your heart in prayer, "Lord, please, do something now."

Pause encourages the thought that life like a roller coaster has up and downs, twists and turns, flying-high times, low times, and busy, hurried flashes and slow, crawling, snail-paced stretches. How can you appreciate the pause as sacred? Find grace in the wilderness? Treat the harshness of the wilderness as a part of God's plan in his sacred work in you? How can you seek God anew in the dung of the wilderness? Trust me; I have not forgotten about sacred dung or the importance of a sacred refrain.

Do you remember where Moses fled after he left Egypt and before God called him to go back to Egypt and lead his people Israel out of Egypt? He fled from pharaoh in Egypt to the wilderness of Midian. Moses rebuilt his life in the shadow of the Good Shepherd's care and became a shepherd himself. He married Zipporah, had a son Gershom, and encountered God on the back side of the desert near Mount Horeb. If a name means anything, and it does, *Gershom* meant *stranger*, or worse yet, *cast away*. Did Moses name his son Gershom because he felt alone; cast away by God, a stranger in a foreign land and a stranger to God?

In Moses' wilderness a bush burned, God spoke, Moses listened to God from the flaming bush, and then he put his name on the dotted line contracting to follow God. Following God is not without a wilderness or risk. "Here I am," Moses said to God's fire in the bush and the rest is history. What's bizarre is that Moses was in his wilderness experience before God chose him to lead the people out of the wilderness. God follows this cycle: revelation, exodus, wilderness, and the promise (or Promised Land). God reveals Jesus. God allows a crisis that requires a pause, a mysterious pause, an exodus of sorts. God sends you down a rope or on the road into the wilderness where He reveals himself afresh. God delivers you by His promise.

Study Jacob at the Jabbok River. Study Rahab in Jericho. Study David's life in battles, in caves, in grief, and on the run. Study the prophets like the agricultural fig picker from Tekoa, turned prophet, Amos. Study Paul's life saved by God's rope, his life on the ropes, and his life holding onto God like a rope and trusting him as he preaches. Study John the Beloved apostle: saved by God's revelation of Jesus, exiled in exodus to Patmos; the mysterious pause becomes a place where flowers bloom in his desert; and the promise of God leads him to write The Revelation. Sometimes the cycle,

revelation, exodus, wilderness, and the promise, repeats itself many times in the course of a lifetime. Embrace the wilderness as a place of grace where God's fire burns fresh in you.

If you ponder this mysterious pause, you discover almost everything worth enjoying possesses a pause: great literature has commas; great writers often have quiet periods before a flurry of creative stories; majestic music flows on musical scores with crescendos and decrescendos spelled by silent pauses; great speeches flow with dramatic effect to grab hearer's attention with interspersed pauses, silence; scientists describe great breakthroughs as coming after long periods of tiring research; great athletes and soldiers train in lonely, wilderness-like agony in preparation for competition or battle. Write this down: One day you will wake up in the dark wilderness and it will be just what the doctor ordered.

By now, you should be asking, "What does a wilderness have to do with dung?" Jesus shared two simple stories about dung. The first story fell in line with a series of brief aphorisms, statements in the context of the cost of following Jesus. Jesus mentions a dunghill. He begins with this familiar statement: "And anyone who does not carry his cross and follow me cannot be my disciple" (Luke 14:27, NIV). He then speaks of counting the cost of building a house before you build and shifts to salt: "In the same way, any of you who does not give up everything he has cannot be my disciple. Salt is good, but if it loses its saltiness, how can it be made salty again? It is fit neither for the soil nor for the manure pile; it is thrown out. He who has ears to hear, let him hear" (Luke 14:33-35, NIV).

Did you see what Jesus said? As a Christian you count the cost of following him. You spice the world up as the savor, the good taste of God's grace. You live as the salt of the earth people sprinkling a little heaven on earth. You salt the tasteless world with the delightful salt of God's grace. If you do not do this, you deserve to be carried out to the dung heap, the dunghill, or, as you just read, the manure pile (*kopria* in Greek). Often, farmers used a dunghill as a place to dump manure from animals and humans. Remember the historian Herodotus from the last chapter who used the Greek word *kopron*, a reference to grain produced by manure spread among the dirt and seeds? Jesus knew of the farmer's dunghill as a dumping ground for fertilizer for crops on future days.

The second story, or story-alongside the story, is known as a parable. The parable Jesus told makes sense if you think about dung as manure for fertilizer. Then he told this parable: "A man had a fig tree, planted in his vineyard, and he went to look for fruit on it, but did not find any. So he said to the man who took care of the vineyard, 'For three years now I've been coming to look for fruit on this fig tree and haven't found any. Cut it down! Why should it use up the soil?' 'Sir,' the man replied, 'leave it alone for one more year, and I'll dig around it and fertilize it. If it bears fruit next year, fine! If not, then cut it down'" (Luke 13:6-9, NIV). The KJV actually says, *dung it*, that is, throw dung around the fig tree and mix it in the soil as nutrients to fertilize it.

Oh, yes! Jesus' declaration appears both practical and spiritual. On the practical level, a fig tree or your yard or a bush or a wilting oak tree, for that matter, might simply need sun, rain, fertilizer, and time to grow. On a spiritual level, a servant of Christ needs grace, prayer, fertilizer in the form of God's Word, and time to mature in Christ.

The mysterious pause is a sacred refrain like those in a ballad or musical score, a phrase, interval, or time when we pause in the action before we return to the action. Given this sacred dung as a sacred refrain, we discern God's grace and the wisdom to carry on or to know what to do next. The spiritual life, like a fig tree, requires dung, fertilizer, time for each of us to bear fruit.

Jesus gives a kind of humorous play on words: dung (*kopron*) is necessary for you to bear fruit (*karpon*). So I offer you this formula: Add *kopron* to your life in Christ to bear *karpon*. Or, Jesus plus a little dung helps you bear fruit in God's kingdom. Or, better yet, a little dung never hurt anyone. After all, dung like a wilderness experience can actually be good for the soul.

Right now as I write in a flurry of fury about a burning bush, a welcome wilderness, and dutiful dung, I find myself in a wilderness experience in the quietness, loneliness, pain, and a mysterious pause. The quietness comes after a period of loud noise, a hectic pace, and a chaotic schedule that wilted my soul like a failing fig tree. The loneliness comes in the lostness, and in the deafening solitude of moving from the life of a pastor always around people to my life as a writer in my office daily alone. The pain comes from an experience where, for lack of a better way of putting it, King Aretas IV instructed the governor and his men showed up with bad news, and I had to escape by the skin of my teeth by ropes down the wall and into the night and off to Arabia.

I am in Arabia now, my wilderness, my time where God spreads dung around my wilting fig tree as much as my soul, to nurture me and fertilize me for His future work in me. The mysterious pause comes with suspense, mystery, fear and faith mixed like dung and dirt, in anticipation of the fresh movement of God's grace. I find myself thinking, "God, what will you do next?" I pray daily pouring out my heart in prayer, "Lord, please, do something now." I search for the sacred in the whiff of the dung, in the darkness of the wilderness, aiming to catch a glimpse of God's burning bush, His holy fire. I know, deep down, the formula works: Add *kopron* to your life in Christ to bear *karpon*; Jesus plus a little dung helps you bear fruit in God's kingdom; a little dung never hurt anyone. After all, dung like a wilderness experience can actually be good for my soul.

It can be good for yours, too. If the Greek historian Herodotus lived today he might warn you that history repeats itself, a circular movement of time producing whirlwind chaos. A scientist might alert you to some continuum convincing you that life thrusts forward toward space in linear time like an airplane flying in a straight line toward its destination in a fixed point in time like observing a timeline in a history or science book. "Life goes in circles. Life goes round and round like a merry-go-round," the circular believer in time might announce. "I can never finish all the things I need to get done. Yesterday, today, tomorrow, my schedule is jammed, overloaded, cram-packed. I am slammed. Times flies," the linear believer in time might proclaim in frustration.

I am not so sure, circular or linear. I do know the Bible speaks of chronology, time as in your dentist appointment on Wednesday at 10:30 a.m. or the seven o'clock meeting or picking up the kids after school at 3:45 p.m. The Bible also speaks of *kairos*, season of time, fruitful times for a purpose, a time when God appoints time for his purpose (Mark 1:15).

Most of all, I tend to believe that my seminary professor Kirkpatrick, *Great Knock*, must have had insight and wisdom and experience: "One day you're going to go through a wilderness experience. One day. Everybody in the ministry goes through a wilderness experience. Everybody needs a wilderness experience." He spun tangled webs of intellectual prowess on process theology which I do not understand, but one thing I can assure you he hinted at: Life is a process. Life happens.

You can no more predict the future any more than you win a million dollars picking lottery ticket numbers or the NCAA men's basketball bracket in March madness. You can no more control life than a scientist can control a meteor zipping and hurling its way through space. You can no more force life than storm chasers can force a tornado in Oklahoma or Texas to stop, land, or turn. Life happens. Surprise happens. Wilderness happens.

In the process of life, you take the bad with the good, the dung with the delight, the wilderness journey with the joy in the journey, and trust God. "In God I trust; I will not be afraid. What can man do to me?" (Psalm 56:11, NIV). "Trust in him at all times, O people; pour out your hearts to him, for God is our refuge" (Psalm 62:8, NIV). "Trust in the Lord and do good; dwell in the land and enjoy safe pasture. Delight yourself in the Lord and he will give you the desires of your heart. Commit your way to the Lord; trust in him..." (Psalm 37:3-5, NIV).

Life is a process where God's hand saves us (revelation), delivers us (exodus), guides us (wilderness), and leads us by his amazing and stunning grandeur of grace (His promise). Life is a process whereby God's grace we learn of His grace and trust his Hand.

I am in Arabia now, thankful for the quietness, loneliness, pain, and a mysterious pause. "Thankful?" you question me. Yes, thankful, because in my weakness God's grace has been made strong in me. In my loneliness I draw near to God and He draws to me in fresh, innovative ways. In my pain the God of the wilderness heals my soul. In the mysterious pause I appreciate the grace so readily available and the peace of God that grants me an open door of access by faith so that I can now rejoice in the glory of God (Romans 5:1-2).

I am in Arabia now, warming my heart next to the flame of a bush that burns, God's holy fire that invites me into the scared. What can I learn? How can I grow closer to God? How can I listen to His still small voice? What can I find as I look into his holy fire? What does God have for me next? How is God preparing me for future service, future ministry, and future extender of the hand of His grace to others as a servant of Christ?

I am in Arabia now, seeking God's face in the fire, seeking His grace, keeping my eye on the prize in life's race. I sense in the depths of the wilderness on the edge of the desert that God's grace has already gone before me. I feel His grace turning the bad things into good things by His grace and for His glory.

Bad things turn into good things by God's grace. I reflect on this in many areas. I ask, "Is this true?" A Swiss manufacturer and builder of steel-case chairs had a problem. The fabric on their chairs proved toxic. In an effort to change, they hired Bill McDonough and a fellow chemist who tested 8,000 chemicals and came up with a solution: new fabric safer for employees in the factory in the manufacturing process, safe enough to almost eliminate all toxicity, and safe enough to eat—an edible fabric. Furthermore, the safe fabric reduced production costs, improved the environment with an environment-friendly product, and left-over fabric scraps produced felt and were sold to Swiss farmers for crop insulation. According to Chip and Dan Heath in their book *Made to Stick*, "The scraps were transformed from hazardous waste into crop insulation."[17] The dung of waste transformed into insulation as fertilizer for future farm crops. Bad things turn to good things.

In Austin, Texas, years ago, the water utility department attempted to solve a problem of sewage sludge. They did so by culling the sludge, re-engineering it, and producing Dillo dirt, a fertilizer-type dirt that you can purchase at Home Depot, take home, dump in your yard, and help green up your lawn. Last summer in Wichita Falls, Texas, and the Texas drought, a similar thing happened. The River Road Waste Treatment Plant began their "toilet to tap" program to reuse millions of gallons of waste treatment water, purify it, and return it to the taps of homes for use in homes. Edible fabric, Dillo dirt, and the "toilet to tap" program remind me, bad things can turn to good.

Did I read somewhere that in Cambridge, England, scientists developed a commercial recycling process that turns empty toothpaste tubes and drink pouches into aluminum and fuel in three minutes? The muck of waste, tubes, and pouches combine to recycle into aluminum for smelting and into hydrocarbons for fuel. Will you

---

17 Chip and Dan Heath, *Made to Stick: Why Some Ideas Survive and Others Die* (New York: Random House, 2007).

think about this next time you brush your teeth or use aluminum? Bad things convert to good things. Cambridge researchers and scientists agree.

Literary author Charles Dickens never would have written one of his best novels, *Bleak House* in 1852, about poor public sanitation if he had not lived through it, felt the sting of child labor in a rat-infested factory sticking labels on jars, and smelled the stench of London mud in the streets, largely feces from horse and human waste. "That 'mud' would disappear," writes Oxford literary scholar John Sutherland, noting, "Six years later (1858), the engineer Joseph Bazalgette began construction of the sewer system under the London streets."[18] The bad mud, in a sense, became a source of social change to improve sanitary conditions in London. Bad things can turn to good things.

For Joseph in Genesis, as we have seen, when his brothers sold him into slavery and he entered prison, and encountered a kind of wilderness of bad things, dung if you will. Yet, the bad turned to good as God used him to save his brothers during famine to show God's grace of forgiveness when

---

18 John Sutherland, *A Little History of Literature* (New Haven: Yale University Press, 2013), 47.

vengeance might well have been expected, and to celebrate "God meant it for good" in retrospect considering God's grace. A bad thing tuned into a good thing.

Moses' exile to the wilderness netted him exile, time, time with God, and renewed purpose in the fertilizer of dung's travail as he then led God's people out of Egypt, miraculously through the Red Sea, through the wilderness, and to the edge of entering God's land of promise. A dark, bad thing in the wilderness, turned into the good thing when you consider God's deliverance by miracle and God's hand by mercy of His grace.

All this carries our discussion back to Paul, to his dung comment ("I count it all dung"), and to Arabia and beyond. "But whatever was to my profit I now consider loss for the sake of Christ. What is more, I consider everything a loss compared to the surpassing greatness of knowing Christ Jesus my Lord, for whose sake I have lost all things. I consider them rubbish, that I may gain Christ..." (Philippians 3:7-8, NIV).

Paul weighed and added up the accomplishments, circumstances, and challenges of his life and declared that compared to Christ it was as rubbish, trash, dung. Paul switches and

intermingles metaphors from dung or rubbish
or household trash, *loss* in a word, to *gain*. Paul's
own wilderness experience, his own quietness,
loneliness, pain, and a mysterious pause, and his
own loss served as personal and spiritual gain.

Paul switches, and intermingles dung with
gain, a banking term indicating *interest earned*. If
dung might be the fertilizer, the time needed for
Paul to mature in his faith, then the hard things
and wilderness journey would certainly mean
that Paul viewed his hardship as gaining or in-
creasing his personal and spiritual interest in
God's kingdom currency. For Paul, a penny saved
was not a penny earned, but a saved pain was interest earned for future service. For him, to lose
meant to gain; to lose in one experience was to
gain in service for a future experience. Paul knew
the dung experience served as fertilizer to equip
him to serve for future days.

Paul knew the formula works and God's grace
works by faith: Add *kopron* to your life in Christ
to bear *karpon*; dung as fertilizer bears fruit. Paul
spells this idea of present or past dung as fertilizer for future ministry in strong, clear tones. He
clarified this formula to the Corinthian Christians,
"Praise be to the God and Father of our Lord Jesus

Christ, the Father of compassion and the God of all comfort, who comforts us in all our troubles, so that we can comfort those in any trouble with the comfort we ourselves have received from God" (2 Corinthians 1:3-5, NIV). God comforts us in pain. God's comfort equips us to comfort others. Bad things might yet equip us to do good things in the light of God's grace.

Paul outlines the good, the fruit Christians deliver: "But the fruit of the Spirit is love, joy, peace, patience, kindness, goodness, faithfulness, gentleness and self-control. Against such things there is no law. Those who belong to Christ Jesus have crucified the sinful nature with its passions and desires" (Galatians 5:22-24, NIV). Did you hear that as you read it? The seemingly bad thing, the cross, yields to the glorious good thing, salvation. The dung of the cross, Jesus' blood and the horrors of crucifixion, surrenders to the dazzling hope of Christ in the resurrection. Between two earthquakes, one small earthquake at the cross and one violent earthquake at the resurrection, Christ rises to equip His saints and servants to overcome the dung, live in His grace, and bear fruit to serve others. The bad thing named the cross of Christ turns into a good thing named the resurrection of the Lord Jesus Christ, or more personally the power of the resurrected Christ in us bearing fruit.

Whether circular time or linear time, whether Paul felt he traveled in ministry around in circles or that time flies, he knew of God's grace and God's hand of grace, even in the dark times, the wilderness times, and the time any single one us might describe as pure dung. Like Paul, we keep our eyes on Jesus, and pray we do not become weary or give up or lose heart.

"Therefore we do not lose heart," Paul encourages. "Though outwardly we are wasting away, yet inwardly we are being renewed day by day. For our light and momentary troubles are achieving for us an eternal glory that far outweighs them all. So we fix our eyes not on what is seen, but on what is unseen. For what is seen is temporary, but what is unseen is eternal" (2 Corinthians 4:16-18, NIV).

And therein lies the challenge; keeping our eyes on Jesus, allowing the dung of the wilderness to fire our souls and fertilize our hearts in time in preparation for future ministry, and differentiating between the temporary and eternal while celebrating God's grace and relishing His joy. By the way, Paul repeats himself over and over in his letters, saying the same thing with different words to drive home his point and passion of grace. His words offer paradoxes: to lose to gain; to feel personal pain to comfort others; to experience wounds to be able to help heal others; to fertilize with stinky dung to produce fragrant, sweet-smelling and honey-tasting fruit; and to enter the darkness of the wilderness to discover the light of God's plan, hand, and sacred grace.

When Paul nears the end of his life, he writes a simple message in one of his letters to Timothy. "I have fought the good fight, I have finished the race, I have kept the faith. Now there is in store for me the crown of righteousness, which the Lord, the righteous Judge, will award to me on that day — and not only to me, but also to all who have longed for his appearing" (2 Timothy 4:7-8, NIV).

Makes you wonder if Paul used the word *fought* remembering the suspense of sliding down the wall on ropes and running for his life to Arabia, the theological battles, the battles in cities like Thessalonica and Ephesus, the battles against Roman culture and oppression, and the battles to save his life from lion-teethed people like King Aretas IV, local Roman authorities, the

Jewish Sanhedrin, shipwrecks, and snake bites on mysterious islands.

Makes you wonder if he used *kept the faith* in a nostalgic twist remembering the first Christians who helped him in Damascus on Straight Street, Barnabas, Peter, James, John the Beloved, Silas, Lydia, Phoebe, the Philippian jailer, and the host of other brothers and sisters in Christ who fought with him in the trenches.

Makes you wonder when Paul used the words "also to all who have longed for his appearing" if Paul imagined a banquet in heaven served up with the fatted calf where he could seek forgiveness finally from Stephen, and tell stories of the battle over iced tea and chicken-fried steak, mashed potatoes, and homemade biscuits with real butter and honey.

Three years in Arabia, fourteen years, fifteen days, the numbers keep coming up in his letters, but I can sure bet you that Paul never forgot the first day or the last day of his walk with Christ. And as often happens, my guess is he remembered more in the first three years than he remembered in the stress and battles of the next ever-how-many years. And my guess is that by the time Paul penned "I have fought a good fight,"

fight transliterated into our English word *agony*. Paul probably felt the weariness of ministry and agony, and he longed for heaven looking forward, but that looking backward with thanksgiving his eyes misted with wet tears thinking of the suspense of Arabia, his mysterious pause in the wilderness, and his journey of grace.

Paul knew where he began in Damascus and ended in the end, heaven would all rest on, as the old hymn goes, God's "Amazing Grace, how sweet the sound..." and a grace greater than all (our) his sin. Grace has a way of arriving at the door of the heart, entering in to save us, deliver us, guide us, and carry us home on the journey if only we throw out the welcome mat, invite her in, and sit down at the banquet joined by family, friends, saints and sinners, and the King.

As for me, as I look back over my life today, I give thanks for my Arabia, my wilderness journeys, and the dew of grace I sipped from heaven's fount in times of agony. And so I leave you with Paul's words, and I choose them as my own written to you: "The God of peace will soon crush Satan under your feet. The grace of our Lord Jesus be with you" (Romans 16:20, NIV). That benediction gives me hope. It reminds me God can turn the bad things into good things. It helps me celebrate the joy of Christ because one day you might wake up in the wilderness and it will be just what the doctor ordered. You will find God afresh, catch the flame of His fire, and live to tell others about it with gratitude at a banquet of joy.

Notes to the Reader

Oh reader. Did you read this chapter and think, "I am in a wilderness now!" Or, "Been there. Done that!" Or, "Never thought about it; I hope the wilderness journey is not in my future."

I must tell you I finished most of this chapter late at night. Rain fell on the roof. Darkness set in. I finished, checked a Facebook post, and discovered I was writing on the anniversary of Dietrich Bonhoeffer's death, April 9, 1945. Today marked the anniversary of his death. In one of his last sermons before the Nazis exiled him to the wilderness of prison, Bonhoeffer spoke words of grace.

Bonhoeffer's death, "his last station on the road to freedom" as Eric Metaxas describes it, came that Monday morning, April 9, 1945. His German captors and prison guards entered his cell in Flossenbürg with an invitation "come with us." His cruel captors hung him and burned his body in a pile with other bodies. Spectators said Bonhoeffer uttered those now infamous words, "This is the end. For me the beginning of life," which sound like the poet T.S. Eliot in his poem *East Coker*, "In my beginning is my end."

However, for Bonhoeffer, in his own words, the beginning is the end and the end is the beginning: "Death is grace, the greatest gift of grace that God gives to his people who believe in him. Death is mild, death is sweet and gentle; it beckons us with heavenly power, if only we realize it is the gateway to our homeland, the tabernacle of joy, the everlasting kingdom of peace."[19]

I brushed my teeth, slipped into bed, rested my head on the pillow, listened to rain fall on the house and drip off the roof, and pondered Bonhoeffer. Eeriness fell over me, my eyes began to mist like the old Apostle Paul, and I thanked God on the pillow for love, life, hope, peace, and grace, including my Arabia of suspense. God's grace drips into our lives as gently as the evening rain.

Oh, reader, did you like my story about C. S. Lewis and my *Great Knock*? We both had

19 Eric Metaxas, *Bonhoeffer: Pastor, Martyr, Prophet, Spy: A Righteous Gentile vs. The Third Reich* (Nashville: Thomas Nelson, 2010), 531.

professors named Kirkpatrick. I am no C. S. Lewis, but I will claim we had a *Great Knock* to challenge our thinking, inform our theology, and electrify our minds.

Oh, I need to tell you something. Do not laugh at me. I have never been camping. I do like to step outside on a spring night or a summer night, and stare at the stars, listen for sounds, and capture the essence of darkness. I love the twinkle in the stars, a meteor shower, and moving airplanes, blinking red lights, and sailing satellites. I love the sound of the ruffle of the leaves in the wind, cicadas singing, crickets chirping, and an occasional blood-curdling scream from a pack of coyotes. I love the darkness and the contrast of dark to light: the stars, a streetlight, or the beam from a headlight coming down the street. Margaret Atwood tells me if I aim to write I must focus on contrasts like darkness and light. She says, "Possibly, then, writing has a lot to do with darkness, a desire or compulsion to enter it, and with luck, to illuminate it, and to bring it back out to the light."[20]

Thank you, Margaret Atwood! Am I a miner mining gold in the dark? Am I a detective trying

20 Margaret Atwood, *Negotiating with the Dead: A Writer on Writing* (Cambridge: Cambridge University Press, 2002), xxiv.

to uncover the clues with a flashlight in the dark? Am I an astronomer peering through a telescope with one eye, hoping to see color and the splash of stars and a cataclysmic collision of particles in space in the darkness?

I have never been camping or camped in the wilderness, but I have tried to sense the darkness minus crawling snakes, sand storms blinding your eyes, wild packs of coyotes breathing down your neck, and scorpions. I have, though, and I suspect, in suspense and the sustaining grace of God, we've all lived through a wilderness experience with both darkness and danger. Like Paul in Arabia and Moses in Midian, we all aim to stretch and reach for God's light as if trying to catch a star.

God's light may awaken you to faith and blind you for a season to arrest your heart to His new light, or He may warm your soul in the flame of His bush, his guiding light. All told, by God's grace one simple goal of sacred dung involves moving out of the darkness, or even the dung, into the light of God's new day. You cannot sit in the darkness forever, or wallow in the dung as if you enjoy it. Get out! Get up! Get moving! Get grace!

Did you like the biblical scholar Lightfoot's *mysterious pause* quote? His word proved simple, concise, meaningful, and helpful. If you find yourself right now in the darkness of the wilderness grasping for God's grace in light, stop for a moment and ask God to speak to you, lead you, and help you learn in the dark what you will later understand in his light. Does that make sense? If that seems too complex, shoot for simplicity: pour out your heart to God like the Psalmist's prayer mentioned earlier from one of my favorite songs (Psalm 62:8). If none of that works, then pray out loud right now, "Lord, remember me. Please, God, what will you do next in my life? Lord, please, do something now."

Grace starts with God's light and progresses in process as we cling to his light in prayer. Life is a process, after all. In discussing the mysterious pause in the wilderness, did you feel rejection, condemnation, self-condemnation, or the loneliness of exile? Have you been there? Are you there now? Do you hate where you are at right now in your life? Does it smell like dung?

I heard a man say once, "Life stinks!" His words reminded me of my sixth-grade year. You want to know this, right? In the early seventies, in the days of hip-hugger pants, long hair, tie-dye shirts, Mod Squad, One Adam-12, and the fading

Beatles and emerging Bee Gees, I played the tambourine in a band. Our band only knew one song: *The Age of Aquarius*. I had no rhythm in those days and upset the band with my out-of-rhythm shaking of the tambourine. The other three guys in the band proved to be fantastic musicians, especially John Graham. Oh, John Graham, where are you? My guess is you made it rich playing the drums in some outrageous band. Can I join you and play the tambourine? John Graham moved to Alabama, I think, but not before his skunk incident. John Graham, drummer, where are you?

John Graham lived in a two-story, red brick, colonial-style house painted white with two big columns guarding the front porch by the walkway to the door. When I visited John one day in his home in the country, I enjoyed my visit in his cool room with drums, and his room plastered with posters on the wall and full of life. John's room felt different than my room in my house because his parents converted their two-car garage into a huge, apartment-like room, wide and spacious. Come to think of it, they probably put John Graham in the garage because they got tired of listening to his drum beating. John could play the drums!

While there, I noticed the black light, the velvet bedspread, the shag carpet, and a small hole in the lower wall where the garage and concrete met. John Graham where are you?

One day in sixth grade John Graham arrived at school and sat down at his desk. Oh, John Graham, what happened to you? "What's that smell?" a classmate muttered reaching to pinch her nose. John Graham responded, "Sorry, a skunk got in my house, in my room." John Graham, where are you? I can still smell that skunk.

Yes, sometimes, life stinks. It smells like the worst part of a skunk, or much like, well, dung, awful dung that you stepped in while walking the dog. What can you do? Ask God to turn the bad thing, dung, into good things, the fragrance of Christ. God masters in turning the bad loss into your good gain. He aims to take the bad darkness of the wilderness and transform it into the light of His good for your good.

Did you like the stories of bad things turned into good things? The edible fabric of the Swiss Steelcase chairs? Edible fabric, Dillo dirt, and the "toilet to tap" program in Wichita Falls, Texas? After you read this and went to get tap water out of your faucet in the bathroom or in the sink, did

Wichita Falls cross your mind, or make you reach for bottled water instead? Did you like the Dickens story of the bad thing, *mud*, changed into a good thing, the drive for underground, healthy public sanitation in London because of *Bleak House*?

I am probably giving you the impression that I know more about Charles Dickens than I really do, but did you know that one of the forces that drove his life and literature was his father? His father wound up in debtor's prison. Because of his father's imprisonment, an eleven-year-old Charles had to enter the world of child labor in a dungeon-like factory. I told you a little about that earlier. A young Charles never forgot that wilderness experience, more than likely never totally forgave his father for messing up his education, his childhood, and incurring shame and embarrassment to Dickens's life.

One of Dickens's biographers described his relationship with his father as the "secret agony of his soul." Psychologists call this a "father wound," a wound that drives some to low self-esteem, self-destruction, or failure, and others to heightened success. For Dickens, the rage against his father drove him to success. Was he trying to prove his father wrong? Please his father? Seek revenge on his father by writing? We can only speculate. We will never fully know. Oxford literary scholar John Sutherland writes of the anguish, suffering, and shame Dickens felt toward his father. He writes, "The scars never healed."[21] If you think about it, Dickens probably thought of his father when he created many of his characters in his novels.

Was the grumpy Scrooge in *A Christmas Carol* really his image of his father? I do not want to go too deep here, but you might say Dickens's childhood darkness in a factory (a very bad thing) helped him shine the light into people's lives by books (a good thing). But with Dickens, I am not willing to go that far, except to say that one thing I have observed: everybody carries a wound of some sort; each of us possess an agony of soul, whether secret or not. Sacred dung invites us into God's light in the darkness, into His oasis of grace in the wilderness, and into His healing grace in the agony of soul. After you escape the wilderness (experience), you should come out on the other side more sensitive to God, more compassionate toward people in the agonies and burdens, and more focused on the light and power of God's grace and goodness.

---

21 Sutherland, *A Little History of Literature,* 117.

"Taste and see that the Lord is good; blessed is the man who takes refuge in him," the Psalmist says. "Fear the Lord, you his saints, for those who fear him lack nothing. The lions may grow weak and hungry, but those who seek the Lord lack no good thing" (Psalm 34:8-10, NIV). Bob Goff in his book *Love Does* wrote, "I used to think that God was good some of the time, but now I know he's good all the time."[22] When God transforms our wilderness circumstances into an oasis of life, we find joy in God's grace. When God shatters the darkness by his light, we find gratitude under the canopy of God's grace. When God turns the bad things into good things, we anchor our lives by His grace.

Did you like the idea of a sacred refrain? Again a refrain on a piece of sheet music or a musical score carries you back to an earlier place in the music. Often in poetry or music the refrain alerts a brief pause, a simple return, and repetitive musical note or chorus of words. In the cantabile, or melodious flow of music, a refrain makes the music flow, memorable, and advances the song on the wings of the chorus. In the cantabile and

22 Bob Goff, *Love Does: Discover a Secretly Incredible Life in an Ordinary World* (Nashville: Thomas Nelson, 2012), 164.

flow of our lives in the darkness, the wilderness, or the dung, a sacred refrain keeps returning us to God's grace, the grace of the cross, His strength, and His goodness. A sacred refrain of grace allows us to know we are not alone, that God's strength is sufficient, and that His goodness can win out in the end. In the sacred refrain, God calls us to grace and carries us forward by His grace. Life is a process, albeit of grace.

I need to tell you this story, blessed reader. I fear you will think I am saying everything in life is good. What we do know is what Paul wrote to the Christians in Rome, "And we know that in all things God works for the good of those who love him, who have been called according to his purpose" (Romans 8:28, NIV). What we don't know, honestly, is that all bad things turn into good things. What we do know is all things can move toward the good under the wings of God's grace. What we don't know either is that all bad things have to stay bad. If such words confuse or conjure up doubt, it's best to refer back to the refrain of God's grace and the mantra of Romans 8:28.

Oh, let me tell you the story. While writing this section I noticed an article about David Copperfield's home. Copperfield, as you know, is a world famous, world-class magician, one who can pull a rabbit out of a hat, supposedly cut women in half in a big box with a big saw, and put them back together again at the end of the show, and escape Houdini-like from chains in an aquarium, submerged in water. Copperfield works the magic.

The other day his house in New York flooded. It seems, the old joke in Associated Press went, the pool vanished. What happened was his roof-top pool leaked and flooded multiple floors of his New York City 57th Street apartment. A malfunctioning pump caused the flood, and no amount of Copperfield magic or abracadabra could fix the pool or dry up the flood waters. It took professionals to repair the pool, dry out floors and walls, and put Copperfield's humpty-dumpty house back together again.

I see irony, but no good or magic in Copperfield's flood. Nor do I see good in an airplane crashing into a French mountainside, Syrian or Egyptian Christians dying at the furor of brutal terrorists, or rescue workers trying to find a missing airplane and missing relatives in the Indian Ocean. In and by themselves, I see no good in any of these tragedies. However, deep down, and lodged deep in my soul while clinging to God, scripture, faith, and grace, I believe in the work of God's grace to take bad things, and somehow plunge the depths to dredge up His good things. How God does it I cannot explain any more than I can explain baseball analytics, astrophysics, history's follies and failures, or the leak from Copperfield's pool.

But what I cannot explain, I can still observe, see, and find the good of God's grace in the darkness, and stretch forth for the light of God's grace toward the good in the wilderness and wildness of an inexplicable life of joy. What I can say with great confidence is this: the bad things in the world, the wilderness journeys in which we wander, and the dung that stinks up our lives, call me to seek God in His grace more than ever before.

I hope Copperfield's house has dried out and the pool works with fresh water again. Do you think he knows it's almost summer? I wonder how far he can see from his rooftop pool in NYC. Do you think he can see into Canada? Do you know God sees him by His grace and also sees you?

This chapter must end. Ernest Hemingway somewhere along the way in my wilderness travels reminded me that writers, like painters, must paint with words. "After you learn to write your

whole object is to convey everything, every sensation, sight, feeling, place and emotion to the reader."[23] At the end of the chapter, I hope to make you feel nostalgia, yours and mine and Paul's at the end of his life longing for a banquet of family and friends in a glad reunion of festive joy.

Did you feel the heaviness, the weight, or maybe become misty-eyed with these words about *fight* and *agony* and the weariness of ministry and the longing for heaven? Can you now, in God's promise by His grace with thanksgiving and eyes misted with wet tears, remember the suspense of Arabia, His mysterious pause in the wilderness, and His journey of grace in you? Can you find it in your heart to thank God for the wilderness, the darkness, and the dung?

Speaking of dung, I must tell you one more story. My apologies, I am not one-hundred-percent sure, but I think preacher Will Willimon told this story in a sermon years ago when I heard him preach. I cannot tell you where. I can tell you he did not preach or tell this story in the wilderness or in the darkness. The light shone.

---

23 Larry W. Phillips, ed., *Ernest Hemingway on Writing* (New York, New York: Scribner, 1984), 51.

The preacher and his daughter sat down at a restaurant in Europe. Whether the city was Lucerne, Switzerland, Rome, Vienna, or a small village in Austria I do not know. But the preacher noticed the scenery, picturesque like postcards sent home to your mother: mountainous in the background, flowers blooming, refreshing air, and romantic in the sense that dreams come true if you ever dreamed of a place to eat in the quiet and picturesque beauty with not a care in the world.

One thing in the story: near the table where the preacher and his daughter ate a meal, flowers cascaded in the background, and colorful flowers decorated the restaurant in a nearby flower pot. A lady who looked like the cook came from the kitchen, wearing a white hat and a white apron soiled from a long day's work. She takes the pitcher in her right hand, walks over to the flowers, and pours. The preacher and his daughter turn their eyes toward the lady and watch. What they thought they would see was water exiting the pitcher, but what they observed in actuality was a red liquid, deep, dark red.

The lady from the kitchen emptied the pitcher, careful to spread the liquid around the flowers, and with a utensil that looked like a wooden cooking spoon to intermingle and mix the liquid in the dirt.

"Ma'am," the preacher quizzed as he called the lady over to the table, "what were you pouring in the flower bed and spreading in the flowers?"

In broken English the lady relied, "Blood. I spread blood around de flowers and in de dirt. It helps them grow."

"Then he [Jesus] told this parable: 'A man had a fig tree, planted in his vineyard, and he went to look for fruit on it, but did not find any. So he said to the man who took care of the vineyard, "For three years now I've been coming to look for fruit on this fig tree and haven't found any. Cut it down! Why should it use up the soil?"

"Sir," the man replied, "leave it alone for one more year, and I'll dig around it and fertilize it. If it bears fruit next year, fine! If not, then cut it down" (Luke 13:6-9, NIV).

And as the story goes, or so I think it goes, a woman had some flowers not flowering and she poured the blood and mixed it as dung with the dirt and the flowers became more beautiful than ever. So if you're in the wilderness, mix in the sacred blood of Jesus with your scared dung and dirt and watch his grace flower as fruit in you!

For when sacred dung mixes with sacred grace in sacred refrain, yesterday's dung becomes preparation for tomorrow's work of God's grace in you and through you.

Turn the page. I have been hinting this nugget of truth for the next chapter on sacred refuge. The nugget: God hurts us to heal us by his grace. Turn the page and explore the sacred.

Sacred Refuge

From Hurt to Healing

Surgeons must be very careful
When they take the knife!
Underneath their fine incisions
Stirs the culprit-Life!

~Emily Dickinson, Poems, "The Poet's Art," number 19[24]

---

24 Emily Dickinson, *Dickinson: Poems* (New York: Alfred A Knopf, 1993), 37.

With ropes we drew up rocks
Hung damp in sea thong, Living mussel.
Under the water grew eglantine,
Standing either for Poetry
Or the saying
"I wound to heal."

~Annie Dillard, *Tickets for a Prayer Wheel*[25]

Write this down: Your pain is not your own.

Occasionally, a man or woman needs a refuge, a place to retreat, a place to unwind, a place to relax for a season, a place to find harbor from the fierce winds of the storm. In the year of our Lord, which I cannot remember, I found that refuge on a cruise to Hawaii. The trip proved simple. Take an airplane from the mainland to Hawaii, catch a cruise ship, unload your one suitcase and backpack, and enjoy seven days and seven nights at sea, on land, and in the sand—a quiet refuge from a busy life.

One stop on the cruise proved unstoppable. We docked in the small harbor called Nawiliwili. If you enter the harbor built in 1930 at the mouth of the beautiful Huleia Stream, you might find

---

25 Annie Dillard, *Tickets for a Prayer Wheel* (Middletown, Connecticut: Wesleyan University Press, 1974), 56.

it recognizable. The nearby beach figures in the movie *Indiana Jones: Raiders of the Lost Ark*. The harbor and beach fit nicely one picturesque section of the Island of Kauai, an island of volcanic origins so named Kauai, *place around the neck*, indicating how a father might carry a child, or *food season*. Folklore for the island's name proves hard to pin down, but adventurers and photographers refer to it as the *Garden Isle*. The beauty stuns. The glory of the beauty mesmerizes.

The Victorian British priest and poet Gerard Manley Hopkins (1844-1889) might well have known something of Hawaii as a child when his father was the British consul general in Hawaii, and published a book on Hawaii. Who knows if he lived in Hawaii, or if his father's book had pictures, but the Oxford graduate devoted his life to two obsessions: the sacrifice of Christ and *spring rhythm* poetry inflected by the grandeur of God, man, nature, and mysticism in the sense of God's creative work, and a human's intimacy with God in the existential struggle for meaning in the madness of reality-hope, physical-spiritual, earthly-eternal. I am not sure if Hopkins's poem *God's Grandeur* reflected on the beauty of Hawaii, but it might well have captured a glimpse of Hawaii's beauty in these words: "The world is charged with the grandeur of God…There lives the dearest freshness deep down things."[26]

Kauai's beauty, elegance, wonder, and adventure attract. *God's grandeur* hails as one clear way to describe it. "Adventure" describes Kauai, too. Hollywood-filmed action movies on the island like *King Kong* (1976), *Jurassic Park* in 1993, *Tropic Thunder*, *Soul Surfer*, and P*irates of the Caribbean: On Strange Tides*. The European explorer James Cook, *Captain Cook*, explored the island, made a map, and died in a fight with the Hawaiians in 1779.

Our cruise arrived in beauty, and in the wake of adventure. A view from the ship captures the island's glory, your own imagination of dinosaurs running in green fields in movies, Harrison Ford's heroic feats, and surfers riding the crest of a wave.

Once off the ship one morning, our family, eleven of us, sought our own adventure. We rented Mopeds. You can rent mopeds, small two-wheeled motorcycles, on the cheap on the island for a fun adventure. We walked to the rental spot, rented our mopeds, received *safety* instructions, and

26 See Rev. Thomas Ryan, Hopkins: *The Mystic Poets Series* (Woodstock, Vermont: SkyLight Paths Publishing, 2004), 57, 1-26.

grabbed our German-style helmets with safety straps for under the chin and began our journey.

"Any ideas on where to ride?" we asked our rental expert.

"Be careful on the main roads, but ride downtown and, if you want, ride down this country road and up the hill toward the canyon. In about two miles you will see cars and parked mopeds. There is a path in the tall trees. Take the path to the waterfall. You will see lots of people there. You can swing on the rope if you like adventure." The rental expert pointed to his left when he described the country road and waterfall.

We decided to begin on the country road and explore the waterfall. The slow speed, the strap under your chin, the wind in your face, the elegiac, cascading canyon, and the crisp air basked in sunshine set the adventure aglow in God's grandeur. Recalling that day now makes me want to return. Recalling the happiness of that day creates longing in me. Recalling the scars cut in my skin that day makes me long for adventure, laugh, and languish over wounds visible, yet invisible.

The rental expert explained the waterfall and muttered something about a Johnny Depp sighting, pirates of the Caribbean, Captain Cook,

and a movie scene filmed at the waterfall. This created curiosity as we arrived at the opening in the tall trees, stopped, parked our mopeds, and ventured into the jungle. Supposedly, one scene from a Pirates movie was filmed at the waterfall. Huge rocks surrounded the waterfall as streams of water flowed over the rocks at the top and into the falls below. The distance from top to bottom appeared to be about forty feet. I noticed men and woman and some children climbing one side of the rock where a man stood to hand them a rope. Once the rope reached an adventurer's hands, the individual leaned on the rope, swung out over the water, released, and splashed down below.

I knew I had to do this. Family members followed. Memories formed in hearts and minds. We repeated this splashing adventure numerous times and returned to our mopeds weary, excited, and anxious for the next stop. One of my daughters needed help starting her moped. I circled back, whisked around beside her, accidentally slid in the mud, and lost control of my moped. As I slid downhill, a barbed wire fence kept me from falling ten feet down a hillside. The barbed wire gripped my lower right arm, sliced it like a knife cutting potatoes, and pierced my upper arm near the shoulder.

Adrenaline pumping my body with strength, I lifted the moped, announced to my daughter I was fine, and proceeded to right the ship, so to speak.

"Your arm! Your arm! You're bleeding!" a lady screamed.

I looked at my arm and noticed three cuts and one deep piercing. My black shirt had also been gripped, ripped, and sliced by the barbed wire. The screaming woman ran over to me, told me to take off my shirt, proclaimed she was a nurse, took my shredded shirt, and made a tourniquet out of it for my bleeding arm. She handed me a long-sleeve, blue t-shirt with red letters and told me to get to the hospital.

I tied the blue shirt around my neck like a Superman cape and started back to the ship down the country road wearing my German-style helmet, swimsuit, my upper torso bare except for the Superman cape around my neck and it flapping in the wind like Superman to the rescue. However, I was the one in need of rescue in the whole comical scene. I made way back to the cruise ship, found sick bay, and received numerous stitches in the three long cuts on my right arm.

The worst part of the accident, I can tell you without question, included a sharp needle and a tetanus shot. I would not need another tetanus shot for ten years after that moment. Yet, I will never forget the moped adventure, the waterfall rope splashes, the arm cuts, and the scars still visible on my right arm to this very day. Wounds form scars. Scars remind us of wounds. Wounds and scars create memory, a reminder of pain, and join together as a symbol of healing.

I figured a trip to Hawaii proves a rare treat, so I wore a long-sleeved, black surfer shirt the rest of the trip, swam in the salt water, and took care of my stitched arm. The mild pain paled in comparison to the fun and adventure. The physician who stitched my arm explained the healing process, instructed me on how to care for the arm to reduce the risk of infection, and told me to have the stitches removed after several weeks by my family physician. Healing took place over time. The stitches came out. The scars remain.

If I had lived in the first century during the days of the Apostle Paul, an altogether different form of medicine might have been used to heal my mangled arm: dung. The prominent Roman naval commander, equestrian, and writer, Pliny the Elder (A.D. 23-79), who died while attempting to rescue a friend at the hands of the monster volcano Mount Vesuvius, wrote in *Natural History*, "Strains and bruises are treated with wild boar's dung gathered in spring and dried. This treatment is used for those who have been dragged by a chariot or mangled by its wheels or bruised in any way. Fresh dung may also be smeared on" (Pliny, *Natural History 28.237*).[27]

My moped accident might have found delicate healing in dried, smeared dung. In fact, the ancient Egyptians, Greeks, and Romans each used dung in various ways to treat wounds, diseases, and to cure ailments. If this sounds absolutely sick or strange, I picked up a newspaper recently and found this headline on the front page: *Cure's Secret: A Gut Reaction.*[28] The small print under the headline caught my attention: "fecal transplants relieve painful colitis, may someday treat obesity."

---

27 Pliny the Elder, as quoted by J. C. McKeown, *A Cabinet of Curiosities: Strange Tales and Surprising Facts from the World's Greatest Empire* (Oxford: University Press, 2010), 73.

28 Seema Yasmin, "Cure's Secret: A Gut Reaction," *Dallas Morning News* (23 January 2015), 1A-2A.

The news article told the story of a woman who had human fecal matter transferred into her bowels as a medicinal cure. I will skip all the details, except to say that the woman had been ill for a long time, and the dung inserted into her bowels helped her gain strength, feel better immediately, and recover her health.

The non-traditional medicinal cure has helped numerous patients in a low-risk, non-surgical, cost-effective, healing remedy for certain forms of colitis. The dung, in a sense, served as healing grace for the once-upon-a-time ailing Indiana woman. What the ancient Egyptians, Greeks, and Romans knew, modern physicians know: dung can heal some ailing individuals and even wounds.

I figured something out in my personal life experience and pastoral journey. Do not feel surprised here. Here is what I figured out: Bad things happen. We're all wounded. Yes, we're all wounded. We all have scars.

Not long ago I read a story about the Boston Marathon bombings of April 15, 2013. In the aftermath of grief, physical injuries, surgeries, wounds, healing, and scars, Dr. Kermit Crawford, a psychologist who lead the Resiliency Center for helping victims and their families, said, "You have to remember, these are normal people dealing with an abnormal circumstance." In the passage of pain, anxiety, stress, insomnia, and recovery in the quest for resiliency, victims and their families still deal with "invisible injuries, unspoken hurts, emotional scars, and invisible wounds." Who knows what lay beneath the skin and scars of human beings? Beneath scars on a right arm? Beneath scars deep below the human hurt, or I mean, the human heart? We're all wounded. Yes, we're all wounded. We all have scars. Most wounds and scars appear unseen, unknown, invisible. This helps me on an excursion, an adventure back to Paul's dung. Paul was wounded. Paul was scarred.

"What is more, I consider everything a loss compared to the surpassing greatness of knowing Christ Jesus my Lord, for whose sake I have lost all things. I consider them rubbish, that I may gain Christ and be found in him, not having a righteousness of my own that comes from the law, but that which is through faith in Christ - the righteousness that comes from God and is by faith. I want to know Christ and the power of his resurrection and the fellowship of sharing in his sufferings, becoming like him in his death... (Philippians 3:8-10, NIV).

Did you see that? Paul aimed to know God's power and share in the fellowship of His sufferings. *Share* means to participate. *Fellowship* means to join a group, to share life, *to join the club*, so to speak. *Sufferings* includes wounds and scars both visible and invisible such as Jesus' nail-pierced hands and feet.

Paul digressed in one of his letters to define and defend his wounds and scars:

> "What anyone else dares to boast about—I am speaking as a fool—I also dare to boast about. Are they Hebrews? So am I. Are they Israelites? So am I. Are they Abraham's descendants? So am I. Are they servants of Christ? (I am out of my mind to talk like this.) I am more. I have worked much harder, been in prison more frequently, been flogged more severely, and been exposed to death again and again. Five times I received from the Jews the forty lashes minus one. Three times I was beaten with rods, once I was stoned, three times I was shipwrecked, I spent a night and a day in the open sea, I have been constantly on

the move. I have been in danger from rivers, in danger from bandits, in danger from my own countrymen, in danger from Gentiles; in danger in the city, in danger in the country, in danger at sea; and in danger from false brothers. I have labored and toiled and have often gone without sleep; I have known hunger and thirst and have often gone without food; I have been cold and naked. Besides everything else, I face daily the pressure of my concern for all the churches" (2 Corinthians 11:21-28, NIV).

Paul's emotional, spiritual, and physical wounds simply could not be avoided in his service to Christ. I cannot speak for Paul, but the idea of wounds substantiated pain, gruesome bloody pangs, and the need for healing that produced scars on Paul's body. Paul uses two Greek words, *rhabdizo*, translated *rods*, and *plege*, translated *plague* or *wounds*. Paul experienced pain at the brutal hands of the Roman lictors in Philippi (Acts 16:22). The Roman lictor carried a bundle of rods with projecting ax-blades and used them to enforce Roman law, public coercion, and to inflict punishment. Paul's pains included shipwrecks, stoning, and the like, but no pain or wounds lanced his body and injured his body like the fierce blows from the military-clad Roman lictors. No doubt Paul's wounds and scars needed a healing touch, a comforting balm, and, possibly, dried dung draped over his wounds for medicinal healing.

If you think you are having bad day, or feel hurt by the wounds, or trapped by past scars, or deep in the dung, you have a friend in Paul and a friend in Jesus. Wounds became grounds for healing. Scars became marks for forgetting and remembering at the same time in an effort to move forward in the wonders and grandeur of God's grace.

Paul spells it out clearly in Galatians 6:17, "I bear on my body the marks of the Lord Jesus." Was he acknowledging a mark of ownership like slaves in ancient days marked by their owners with a tattoo-like wound that scarred, a stigmata from stigma meaning a mark? Was he confessing his fellowship with Jesus' sufferings as a stigma, a mark of fellowship with his wounds? Was he declaring the pain of the visible and invisible wounds of his own life, asking Christ to heal them, and to help him remember God's grace every single time he looked at his own scars?

If you combine Paul's wounds, scars, and healing requirements, they take us from his fellowship in the sufferings of Christ to his personal thorn in the flesh. Paul grieved over and yet accepted his thorn in the flesh. Paul describes the wound, "To keep me from becoming conceited because of these surpassingly great revelations, there was given me a thorn in my flesh, a messenger of Satan, to torment me. Three times I pleaded with the Lord to take it away from me. But he said to me, 'My grace is sufficient for you...'" (2 Corinthians 12:7-9, NIV). Bible scholars speculate Paul's Damascus road experience in a flash of light caused him to have blurred vision, an eye problem, and the medical words might indicate such an optical allusion.

No one could prove the eye theory, but it makes sense. What makes more sense is that Paul appears to indicate a thorn from a rose, maybe the Eglantine rose of ancient Rome, Greece, and Europe. The rose appeared double-edged, a sweet fragrance pleasant to the nostrils and, according to its namesake, also *prickly*, a *briar*, often referred to as the *sweet briar*. Paul knew the wounds and scars of his faith in Christ possessed *sweetness* as well as *prickliness*, yet he learned to gain strength from Christ in the good and bad, in the sweetness and the prickliness, and among the roses and the thorns.

Even in the bad things, Paul discovered God's good things. Even in hardship, Paul longed for fellowship with Christ. Even among the prickly thorns, Paul yearned to smell the sweet fragrance of Christ. In piles of dung-like experiences of pain, Paul desired the healing grace of Jesus Christ.

Had Paul learned from the Old Testament Scriptures from the bones of Joseph, and from his reconciliation with his brothers of the power of God's healing grace? Joseph had instructed his family to take his bones from Egypt and carry them home. In an unusual verse in the Bible see this: "Moses took the bones of Joseph with him because Joseph had made the sons of Israel swear an oath. He had said, 'God will surely come to your aid, and then you must carry my bones up with you from this place'" (Exodus 13:19, NIV). And next we hear of Joseph's bones buried in Shechem: "And Joseph's bones, which the Israelites had brought up from Egypt, were buried at Shechem in the tract of land that Jacob bought for a hundred pieces of silver from the sons of Hamor, the father of Shechem. This became the inheritance of Joseph's descendants" (Joshua 24:32, NIV).

Joseph's bones represent the man, his mission, and his life just like British King Richard III's bones found recently in Leicester, England, buried beneath a church parking lot, or the bones of writer Miguel de Cervantes found in a convent in Madrid, Spain. The bones represent the man. What about Joseph, the man? The writer of Hebrews informs us. Joseph lived by faith: "By faith Joseph, when his end was near, spoke about the exodus of the Israelites from Egypt and gave instructions about his bones" (Hebrews 11:22, NIV).

Apparently, according to Hebrews, all you need to know about Joseph is that he lived by faith. If we speculate that Paul wrote the letter to the Hebrews, which I will do, then we can say with confidence that Joseph's faith was Paul's faith and vice versa. If bones tell us about the man, then the bones planted in Shechem in the dust, dirt, and dung, if you will, must be the bones of a man of faith. Make no bones about it!

Joseph's DNA swirled in cells of faith in God, and followed a pattern, one mentioned in the last chapter: revelation, exodus, wilderness, and the promise (or Promised Land). Joseph learned of

God by revelation, God's care, God's shepherding care, and faith at the feet of his father Jacob as a child. Although flawed, Jacob wrestled with God and the *kopron* (dung) of his *karpon* (fruit) later caused him to mature in his own faith. Joseph learned enough as a boy from his father Jacob to trust in God as his refuge in the bad and the good.

Joseph himself experienced an exodus: sold into slavery by his brothers and slavery itself. Joseph's wilderness experience might well have included stints in prison, loneliness, longing for the joys of home, and exile in a land where he had to adjust to an entirely different culture, language, and customs, and make his way independent of a strong base of support. Joseph's promise (Promised Land) could be written both in biography and bones as a serendipity of faith, the mysterious hand of God guiding him, protecting him, blessing him, and carrying him to a position like vice president of Egypt where he was second in command to the Pharaoh. The Lord was with Joseph (Genesis 39:23), and if Joseph had known the Psalms like the Apostle Paul did during his day as an *Israelite indeed*, then Psalms like these two spoke to the core of the heart and soul: "The Lord is a refuge for the oppressed, a stronghold in times of trouble. Those who know your name will trust in you, for you, Lord, have never forsaken those who seek you" (Psalm 9:9-10, NIV); and "God is our refuge and strength, an ever-present help in trouble. Therefore we will not fear, though the earth give way and the mountains fall into the heart of the sea, though its waters roar and foam and the mountains quake with their surging" (Psalm 46:1-3, NIV).

Whatever faith Joseph possessed, he must have felt fear, watched the waters rise up to his neck, and worked hard at keeping his feet underneath his body and soul, wounds and scars, when his life quaked. Joseph must have had a good sense of God, his care as refuge, and God's unique ability to provide mercy and grace in the nick of time. Joseph must have had faith in God as a refuge and strength, a very present help in time of trouble.

People of faith have faith in fear, keep swimming by faith when the flood waters rise, and know how to keep their feet and head steady when all else around them shakes. I think of Joseph's bones, his faith, and his leadership. I once read that the late and legendary NFL football coach of the Dallas Cowboys, Tom Landry, once said of a good leader, "A leader is a person who keeps his or her head when everybody else is losing theirs." Joseph kept his head and his heart in God his refuge.

I do not have to tell you the rest of Joseph's story of faith, you already know it. You know about God's promise of provision for him, how God used Joseph to provide for the land including his own family during an awful famine, and how God reconciled in the grace of forgiveness, Joseph to his brothers, amid a banquet served at the table of forgiveness with food, conversation, laughter, and tears of joy. Nothing better describes a God-kind-of-fellowship than a banquet, food, conversation, laughter, and tears of joy.

Joseph's faith carried him and won the day. Joseph saw his father Jacob again, too. They rejoiced over a reunion of years, the fellowship of many sufferings, and Jacob blessed Joseph and his sons in the power of the Mighty One, the almighty, the Shepherd, the Rock of Israel, and the God who helps you (Genesis 49:24-25).

Joseph had lived through the dungeon of prison, the dung heap of famine, and the dung of alienation—all bad things—to glory in God's grace of freedom, renewal, and restoration in the glory of God's good things. After his father Jacob died, Joseph's brothers worried that he would seek revenge for their intended harm. However, Joseph's faith by grace healed the wounds and covered the scars. And this is what you already know: "But Joseph said to them, 'Don't be afraid. Am I in the place of God? You intended to harm me, but God intended it for good to accomplish what is now being done, the saving of many lives. So then, don't be afraid. I will provide for you and your children.' And he reassured them and spoke kindly to them" (Genesis 50:19-21, NIV). Did you see that? God meant it for good. God's grace rotated the bad things toward his good.

This was one of those moments for Joseph, pure and crystal clear and magical like English writer Gordon Keith Chesterton's magical words. GK once fiercely proclaimed with a prophetic voice like Joseph's in Genesis, "And the more I considered Christianity, the more I found that while it established a rule and order, the chief aim of that order was to let the good things run wild." GK also added, "...joy is the gigantic secret of the Christian."[29] God's good things run wild when

---

29 G. K. Chesterton, Orthodoxy: *The Classic Account of a Remarkable Christian Experience* (London: John Lane The Bodley Head, 1908; repr., Colorado Springs, Co: Shaw Publishers, 2001), 140-41, 243.

placed in His hands, when you trust in Him, and run to Him for refuge in the trail of bad things.

In the wilderness dungeon (I'm in Arabia now!) of my own prison, the dung heap of my own famine, and the dung of my own alienation—all bad things—I have learned by faith in God to glory in God's grace of freedom, renewal, and restoration in the glory of God's good things. I have learned much about faith in the wilderness and dung, among wounds and scars, and in the path of wandering and wondering about God's future plan for me.

Faith requires risk like an adventurer grabbing a rope and swinging over a waterfall and into the splash of water below. Faith presses us forward toward the light in the darkness of the wilderness. Faith in Christ helps us let go of the thorns and enjoy the rose in the pain of life. Faith steps in the dung at times, but shakes its feet free of the dung by grace. Faith feels the bad of a wound, but knows of God's grace to turn the wound into a beautiful, albeit good scar. Faith moves from hurt to healing. Faith accepts the bad through the lens of God's grace to reveal His good. God meant it for good.

"Now faith is being sure of what we hope for and certain of what we do not see. This is what the ancients were commended for. By faith we understand that the universe was formed at God's command, so that what is seen was not made out of what was visible" (Hebrews 11:1-3, NIV). Faith makes visible the invisible, possible the impossible in God's hand of grace.

Famed and retired baseball pitcher of the New York Yankees Mariano Rivera describes his unlikely road into major league baseball, the twist and turns, the trials and tribulations, and the pain and adversity of life, even the pain of losing a friend in his homeland. Known as *Mo* and *Sandman*, the pitcher grew up in a poor fishing village of Puerto Caimito in Panama. He rose from the minor leagues to become baseball's best relief pitcher ever. Mariano's life of success followed a road of hardship, hard work, hard days when the young commercial fisherman turned professional baseball player by trusting God's hand by faith in grace and overcoming life's dung, if you will.

He once said, "Even in a room overstuffed with pain and adversity, the Lord's blessings, and people's goodness, are everywhere, and I am so much richer for having been there."[30] "There" indicates the adverse road, the hardship, the bad things. Rivera still viewed life through God's eyes as a blessing filled with his good, the good things, and good people. God's grace enriches life.

Olympic hero and military veteran Louis Zamperini pledged God's good, hope, resiliency, and the faith not to give up or give in life's dark, dung-like, dungeon moments when all hope seems lost. The book *Don't Give Up, Don't Give In: Lessons from an Extraordinary Life* by Louis Zamperini and David Rensin signals hope for all of us as we grind through the tough parts of life and celebrate the joy of God's grace. Louis Zamperini delivered two helpful words. First, "Sometimes what we see as a loss turns out to be a gain, and sometimes a gain is a loss. I try not to be too swift to pass judgment on any situation, preferring instead to be patient and take the long view because I believe in the end all things work together for good."[31]

---

30 Mariano Rivera with Wayne Coffey, *The Closer: My Story* (New York: Little, Brown, and Company, 2014), 248.

31 Louis Zamperini and David Rensin, *Don't Give Up, Don't Give In: Lessons from an Extraordinary Life* (New York: Dey St., an imprint of William Morrow Publishers, 2014), 164.

Second, author David Rensin tells about a note left in the cover of his own copy of *Unbroken* about Louis Zamperini's life by Laura Hillenbrand. The note, placed next to Zamperini's signature, copied a quote from naturalist and environmentalist John Muir, "Climb the mountains and get their good tidings. Nature's peace will flow into you as sunshine flows into the trees. The winds blow their own freshness into you and the storms their energy, while cares drop away from you like the leaves of autumn."[32] Climbing the mountain of faith yields the sunshine, energy, freshness, and peace of God's grace.

Wound and scars, faith and grace, and bad things turned into good things, though, does not complete the story. If God graces us, and He does, then He calls us to grace others. If God allows pain, wounds, and scars, He begs us to use our experience and experiences to help others. If God wounds us, He wounds us to heal us so that we might heal others.

The priest Henri Nouwen invites the wounded, scarred, and faith-filled Christian to join in the sufferings, not only of Christ, but in the sufferings

---

32 Louis Zamperini and David Rensin, *Don't Give Up, Don't Give In*, 230.

of others. He once penned these words, "He is called to be the wounded healer, the one who must look after his own wounds but at the same time be prepared to heal the wounds of others."[33] He speaks as a minister, but in truth, God's grace calls all of us to heal the wounds of others in compassionate care by grace.

We surrender our personal suffering to God, place our lives in His hand, seek Him as refuge, and understand our lives can help and heal others. We demonstrate compassion like Jesus. We express love, joy, peace, and other fruits of the Spirit to ease life's pain. We pray with people in their adversity and on his or her journey. Our words express simplicity, "Lord, be a refuge, a present help in time of trouble. Lord, be a refuge for the oppressed, a stronghold in times of trouble." We minister encouraging words, soft comfort, and a good thing like compassion in the bad thing happening in another's misery or uncertainty. God's hand of grace embraces us and causes us to extend grace with our hands to others.

The grace shines light. Nouwen adds that grace "turns our mourning into dancing"; and the

---

33 Henri J. M. Nouwen, *The Wounded Healer* (New York: Doubleday, 1979), 82.

light shines for others, too, when we become per-
sons who are transparent, nurturing, understanding, and we allow God's light to shine through us
and to speak through us. He further says, "The
gospel liberates us from the chain of wounds and
needs by revealing to us a compassion that can do
more than react out of the needs that grow from
our wounds."[34] In other words, we learn by faith
in Christ under the wings of His grace, not to self-
ishly cover ourselves and hide in our wounds, but
to spread our wings, to reach out, and to care for
others in our wounds for the sake of Christ. See,
your pain is not your own.

Healing grace in hurting only proves half of
the story. God hurts us to heal us to help heal others by grace through us.

Your pain is not your own. If you follow
Christ, you enter into the fellowship of His sufferings. His pain is your pain. Your pain is Christ's
pain if you consider He sympathizes with our
weaknesses, temptations, struggles, wounds,
scars, and offers healing grace (Hebrews 4:15). In
the pain of our wounds and the weakness of our
scars we look to Christ for strength. "Let us then

---

34 Henri J. M. Nouwen, *Turn My Mourning to Dancing*
(Nashville: Word, 2001), 87.

approach the throne of grace with confidence, so that we may receive mercy and find grace to help us in our time of need" (Hebrews 4:16, NIV).

Your pain is not your own. Your pain, shared in Christ's sufferings, equips you to ease the pain of others. Your wounds prepare you to heal others' wounds. Your scars make ready for your service to place a salve on others' scars. The pain of your thorns offers hope for the sweet rose of healing grace to others.

It's possible, quite possible, that in the dung, the weary angst of the wilderness, and in the pain of thorns that you feel sorry for yourself. A party of pity paints no rosy picture for your future. What can you learn from the dung? What can you investigate about God and yourself, even others in the wilderness? What lesson, truth, special serendipity, or gift can you find in the pain of thorns that you can then offer to another as a rose?

No one will tell you, but pain sticks to all of us; the wounds are real; the scars might be covered like mine right now on my right arm beneath the long-sleeved white Polo shirt I am wearing. Do not fool yourself. Jesus felt the pain on the cross. Paul knew it in lashes on his back, torn emotions of spiritual breakthroughs, and rocks flying at his nose that sent him on the run. Joseph, too, in prison and in longing for home, felt the pangs of pain deep in his soul.

You might feel them right now. In your uncommon experience of pain, even unique to you whatever your circumstances, feel what you feel. Much of what you feel is common and uncommon at the same time. Even the Psalmist felt feeling in the shadows of faith:

"I cried out to God for help; I cried out to God to hear me. When I was in distress, I sought the Lord; at night I stretched out untiring hands and my soul refused to be comforted. I remembered you, O God, and I groaned, I mused, and my spirit grew faint. Selah. You kept my eyes from closing; I was too troubled to speak. I thought about the former days, the years of long ago; I remembered my songs in the night. My heart mused and my spirit inquired: 'Will the Lord reject forever? Will he never show his favor again? Has his unfailing love vanished forever? Has his promise failed for all time? Has God forgotten to be merciful? Has he in anger withheld his compassion?'" (Psalm 77:1-9, NIV).

What the Psalmist felt, Jesus felt, Paul felt, and Joseph felt. The Psalmist, though, much like Jesus, Paul, and Joseph, felt the pained feeling and turned heavenward toward the Lord: "Then I thought, 'To this I will appeal: the years of the right hand of the Most High.' I will remember the deeds of the Lord; yes, I will remember your miracles of long ago. I will meditate on all your works and consider all your mighty deeds. Your ways, O God, are holy. What god is so great as our God? You are the God who performs miracles; you display your power among the peoples. With your mighty arm you redeemed your people, the descendants of Jacob and Joseph" Psalm 77:10-15, NIV).

In pain the Psalmist appealed to God for help. In the pain of the cross Jesus cried out to God for forgiveness for others. In pain Paul entered into fellowship with God as a means of putting the past (dung) behind and pressing toward the future (fruit). In pain Joseph trusted God and worked his way by God's grace as a means of stewardship to God, the Egyptians, citizens in famine, and his own family in the crunch of a crisis.

If bad things happen, and they do, God puts his people on earth to spread His good. Jesus died for love of the good things attached to God's glory. Paul described the good things clearly to the church at Rome: "Love must be sincere. Hate what is evil; cling to what is good. Be devoted to one another in brotherly love. Honor one another above yourselves. Never be lacking in zeal, but keep your spiritual fervor, serving the Lord. Be joyful in hope, patient in affliction, faithful in prayer. Share with God's people who are in need. Practice hospitality" (Romans 12:9-13, NIV). Joseph delivered the good and the goods in good tiding to bring joy to all people.

For the Psalmist, the good things connected to God, His character, and His grace. "Taste and see that the Lord is good; blessed is the man who takes refuge in him" (Psalm 34:8, NIV). For Jesus, the good things fit in the glory of sacrifice, salvation, and service, demonstrated no less than on the cross. Every good tree bears good fruit (Matthew 7:17). For Joseph, God's good in him resulted in good deeds, noble service, and shepherding care for people in their needs. Joseph lived by faith and shared the good things from his nurturing and forgiving heart (Hebrews 11:22).

And all this leads me to you, to your hurt, wounds, and scars. I would never say God forced pain and wounds on you any more than I would say it was God's fault that I slid down a muddy hill and cut my right arm on barbed wire trying to help my daughter. I would not in boldness declare God had the path of my moped accident mapped out any more than I would say that in my human sinfulness I deserved to bleed bloody rivers down my arm that day. Neither would I say that the barbed wire had been waiting for me like an evil demon, ready to slice my arm like a tomato. I think sometimes we tend to over-think so much of life: pain, wounds, scars, moped accidents, and twisted tales of life when we would be better off enjoying the beautiful scenery, accepting that bad things happen, mature in the dung of the bad in hopes of bearing future fruit, and to use the pain, no pain no gain, to minister to others. In the pain, wounds, and scars, seek God as a refuge. In the refuse and refrain of pain in its wilderness, seek God as the refuge for your life.

People I have known who have made the biggest difference in life, and that I have admired most, tend to be those who have overcome bad circumstances and used those experiences by God's grace to help others: soldiers returning from war; athletes overcoming obstacles; businessmen and women succeeding after failure;

ministers sticking with God, people, and a church to see spiritual victories; cancer patients in cancer wards fighting chemotherapy and destructive runaway cells; rescue workers risking neck and limb to save others; researchers on long nights and journeys to cure disease; and social activists seeking to improve living conditions for the poor. In pain we relish grace, and once the wounds scar we find ourselves extending grace to others in the grace of Jesus. The hurt find healing in God's shepherding grace and use it to heal themselves, to help others, and to become a balm of healing for others in their pain.

What follows then becomes a song of joy, a celebration of joy, and a festive feast of joy in Christ. Joy birthed in pain enters the circle of humanity that causes us to join in fellowship. The medicine of joy in pain serves as a prescription for healing and health to heal others. Joy's triumph shared in fellowship and as a medicine to heal others gives pause for gratitude because of God's grace. It also gives cause to watch joy and grace multiply, to spread the world with God's good things.

Yes, bad things happen, but God's servants find His good and sprinkle the world with the glitter of His good things. Paul's good fight for the faith (1 Timothy 6:12) included words as a mentor to a young Timothy, words of God's good in good deeds, good ministry, good reputations, and to love that which is good.

Your pain is not your own. Christ shared in it. You fellowship in it. You understand it. You share it. You lessen the burden of others' pain.

So there you have it, the dung is not all bad. One of my seminary students said construction workers used dung to build his house in India. The bad dung served a good purpose: a roof over his head and wall-like or brick-like dung as insulation for the house. Dung beetles in South Africa roll pieces of cow dung as part of their core diet, and as a way to stay cool, and keep their feet safe while walking across the desert where temperatures can rise to 150 degrees. The beetles, according to *National Geographic*, also use the dung balls as gifts for their mates in mating season. See, the dung is not all bad.

A lady reached the ripe age of 116 not long ago. She lived in Camden, Arkansas. Born to sharecropper parents, she had seen much change, much bad, and much good in her life. Gertrude

Weaver was asked, "What advice would you give to someone to live a long life?"

She pondered the question in her mind, held a flower in her hand, and surmised, "Use a lot of skin moisturizer, treat everyone nice, love your neighbor and eat your own cooking. Don't eat at fast-food places."[35] She offered good advice, although I am not so sure if she had ever eaten at Chick fil A. She might change her mind on the fast-food-places part. Can I add anything to her advice? Sure. Hurt, but heal to help by God's grace. Buy the person's meal in front of you at the drive-through line at Chick fil A. Spread the good things, God's good things. And, finally, if you see an old guy riding a moped with three scars on his right arm on an old country road, encourage him to please, please, be careful. Spread good news and good things in the good of God's grace.

Notes to the Reader

Well, reader, that chapter turned out to be much deeper than I anticipated. At one point I had to stop, reflect on my own wounds deeper than

35 "Oldest Person Dies After Taking Title," *Dallas Morning News* (7 April 2015), 3A.

the scars on my right arm, and thank God for the scars. Life gets complicated, trust me.

Oh precious reader, did you like my story about the Garden Isle, the moped accident, and the funny Superman cape ride with me wearing a German-style helmet on the way to have a doctor stitch my bloody arm? I am looking at my right arm right now. The length of two scars appears to be two inches while the other measures three inches or longer. I look at the scars, remember the Garden Isle, wish I was there now, and am grinning ear to ear remembering the whole bloody episode. The family still laughs at the picture of me riding down the country road in Kauai with a helmet, Superman cape, and tourniquet on my arm. See, your pain is not your own. It is shared, even if in laughter.

In case you have not figured this out, I like the mystic poet Gerard Manley Hopkins and poetry. Reading poetry fires my brain like blueberries, and ignites my creative imagination. Austrian neurologist and psychoanalyst Sigmund Freud once quipped, "Everywhere I go I find a poet has been there before me."[36] Hopkins's poetry speaks of

---

36 John Sutherland, *How Literature Works: Fifty Key Concepts* (Oxford: Oxford University Press, 2011), 99.

Christ (*The Windhover*), the cross, and he speaks clear words in mystical language that resonates with me: "Let all God's glory through" and "we are wound with mercy round and round" and "across my foundering deck shone a beacon, an eternal beam."[37] As a pastor, he highlights God's glory. As a priest, he yields a voice of compassion and mercy. As a poet, he shines God's light like a beam on a boat's deck in the darkness of night.

By the way, I have never seen Harrison Ford in *Raiders of the Lost Ark*, nor have I seen any *Pirates of the Caribbean* movies. Do you think it strange that Hollywood produced a movie about the Caribbean on an island in Hawaii? I did see Harrison Ford portray baseball executive Branch Rickey of the Brooklyn Dodgers in the movie *42: The Jackie Robinson Story*. Robinson played major league baseball as the first African American to play in major league baseball's *big leagues* on April 15, 1947, at Ebbets Field before a crowd of 26,623 spectators. Robinson broke the racial barrier and opened doors for others to follow. Breaking the barrier was not without pain. His pain was not his own.

---

37 Ryan, Hopkins: *The Mystic Poets Series,* 51, 70.

Harrison Ford's character, the cigar-chomping, glass-rimmed, hat-wearing Branch Rickey says, "The world's not so simple any more. I guess it never was. We ignored it. Now we can't." After telling Jackie Robinson he needs a player with guts, the guts to fight back, Rickey informs Robinson, "Your enemy will be out in full force. But you cannot meet him on his own low ground." Rickey presented Robinson with number "42" and the rest is history. Every April 15, Major League Baseball players each wear number 42 in honor of Robinson.

You will not believe this, but yesterday, when I looked at the calendar as I wrote, the black letters on a red page on my phone showed me: APRIL 15. MLB baseball players including my favorite team the Texas Rangers wore number 42 on their jerseys yesterday. You know April 15 as tax day; the day the huge ship Titanic sank in the North Atlantic Ocean on April 15, 1912; and the anniversary of the Boston Marathon Bombing on April 15, 2013. From racism to tax problems to people drowning in debt and despair to the pain, agony, and horrors of grief, life riddles us with bad things that long for a return to the good.

Did you cringe when I talked about the bad thing, the wounds, the *rhabdizo*, in Paul's life: rods to his back by the brutality of the Roman lictors? The Romans scourged, or *flogged* Jesus, that is, whipped Him with whips that more than likely had bone or metal tied to the end. Paul knew pain. Jesus took on pain. Both remind us: their pain was not their own. Paul paved the way for the spread of Christianity. Jesus kicked the door open for Christianity on the cross before Paul could begin his walk and journey on the path of faith.

Oh dear reader, did you identify with the eglantine rose, sweet to savor in the nostrils, but *prickly*, painful, cutting like barbed wire slicing your arm? In life, by God's grace, we have to take the bad with the good, the rose with the thorns, and find a way to press toward God's good. For the record, we used to have a rose bush in the flower bed in front of my house, but the deer kept eating the roses. They left the thorns. Only deer can take life with roses minus the thorns. You cannot...neither can I. Roses, thorns, pain, and wounds prompt my soul to find the grace of gratitude among life's colorful roses, and to find God's healing grace in life's painful thorns.

What about bones? Did you wonder when I told you the barbed wire sliced my arm if the cut went down to the bone? While I was writing this chapter, authorities placed King Richard III's bones in the Leicester Cathedral in a dignified burial after a horse and cart carried his bones to the cathedral. Some dear saint, poet laureate Carol Ann Duffy, read a poem that began with these lines: "My bones, scripted in light, upon cold soil, a human Braille." Apparently, King Richard III (1452-1485) had lived most of his life in pain, his bones unveiling a known truth: he had scoliosis, a curvature of the spine, that caused him to walk, hunched over, a pain in the bones in his back.

While I was writing this chapter, archaeologists in Spain looked for Cervantes's body dug deep in the cold soil in a convent basement to reveal his bones. They were still checking his DNA, but the quixotic exploration excited the bone-digging, rubber-gloved explorers hoping to unveil a literary giant's bones. You do know that he framed the infamous phrase, *tilting at windmills*, indicating those who take on imaginary adversaries.

Like King Richard III, we all carry pain, and like Cervantes we all face imaginary, even real adversaries. Joseph knew both the realities of pain, adversaries, and the hope of God's revelation, exodus, wilderness, and promise, even the promise of forgiveness. I have known people with chronic pain, but for most, our pain is short-lived, time-tested, and can be turned heavenward to find the grace of God's good. Joseph's bones speak of his faith in God's grace from the grave. Bad things can fit us for God's good things. As for King Richard III and Cervantes, I cannot tell you what their bones speak from the grave. What will yours one day speak?

Did you like that Chesterton quote about "the good things run wild?" I have a sense if you follow Jesus, do not sit too long in the dung, or wallow in the dung, you will find the fertilizer and fruit of life's dung in God's good things. God's people open their hearts and His good things run wild in them, and then run wild in the world to help heal others' pain.

Here I go with another poet again. Nobel Laureate Czeslaw Milosz, a man who witnessed the destruction of Lithuania and Poland during World War II, writes in agony and poetically of the grief of his witness. The time in his life cast a cloud over his life, horrid, gloomy, dung-like. He writes, "There are days when people seem to me a funeral of marionettes dancing at the edge of nothingness."[38]

In the darkness, the downward spiral of destruction's bitter days, he writes, "yet we believed that some of us had received a gift, a grace, to spite the force of gravity."[39] He designates himself: "One might say I am a chaplain of the shadows."[40] I cannot say with complete confidence all that Milosz meant by *chaplain of the shadows*, but possibly to say that in the nothingness he aimed to comfort people with the life of *somethingness*, grace; that in the grip of gravity's downward spiral he aimed to launch their lives toward eternity's grip of grace; and that in the dark-shaded shadows he aimed to cast the light of God's grace.

A good chaplain of the shadows assists people in finding a way out of the nothingness, out of the downward pull toward the dung, and out of the darkness. A good chaplain of the shadows God calls each of us to be, a person who turns painful things into good things, spreads God's good

---

38 Czeslaw Milosz, *Second Space: New Poems* (trans. Robert Hass; New York: HarperCollins, 2004), 37.

39 Milosz, *Second Space*, 51.

40 Milosz, *Second Space*, 9.

things, and sprinkles the world with the salt of grace.

Maybe Muir's quote, signed by Louis Zamperini in a note left in the cover of the copy of *Unbroken* given to his friend, does put it best, "Climb the mountains and get their good tidings." Better yet, we have to climb out of the dung. Still better, by grace we climb the mountains of faith and move from hurt to healing, from pain to chaplain in the shadows assisting others in their pain. "I became a servant of this gospel by the gift of God's grace given me through the working of his power" (Ephesians 3:7, NIV).

If Milosz informs me that I am a chaplain in the shadows to call forth the grace of God's light, then Henri J. M. Nouwen signals to me that my pain is not my own. God shapes us, molds us, and crafts us in the contours of His grace to bear fruit. We arrive by grace at the door of opportunity to enter into the suffering of Christ in fellowship and in the sufferings of others.

Nouwen proclaims us *wounded healers*. God wounds us to heal us and we heal others in the shadow of grace. If ever wounds and scars stick to the arm or leg or back or soul, these wounds and scars speak like Jesus' wounds, Paul's scars, or

Joseph's bones. They speak of grace by faith and faith by grace in the cold soil and warm days of life, in wounds and scars, on sunny days in garden isles and on days when dark clouds move in.

I need to tell you about the weather. Clouds form in the distance. Bluebonnets sprinkle the earth like grace. Unlike roses, no thorns crawl on the stems of bluebonnets. The weatherwoman says that our chances of rain appear good. Rain will end our Texas drought. Good things can overpower the bad like rain ending a drought. Now, where was I?

Oh yes reader, wounds and scars mixed in with the fellowship of Christ's suffering like dung and dirt can bear fruit. The fruit is joy. For all the bad stuff Paul encountered, for all the pain he felt, for the wounds that scarred his body, he still found God as his refuge.

Jesus knew of God's protection under grace: "He who dwells in the shelter of the Most High will rest in the shadow of the Almighty. I will say of the Lord, 'He is my refuge and my fortress, my God, in whom I trust.' Surely he will save you from the fowler's snare and from the deadly pestilence. He will cover you with his feathers, and under his wings you will find refuge..." (Psalm 91:1-4, NIV).

Paul sensed God's presence by faith: "But my eyes are fixed on you, O Sovereign Lord; in you I take refuge..." (Psalm 141:8, NIV). Joseph understood God's power in joy: "For you have been my refuge, a strong tower against the foe" (Psalm 61:3, NIV). The joy of the Lord is your strength (Nehemiah 8:10).

All you have to do in the dung is hold your nose and open your eyes to see God's presence, protection, and power; to see his strength as a refuge for you by faith, under grace, in the hope of his joy. Frederick Buechner once penned these brilliant words, "Joy is where the whole being is pointed in one direction, and it is something by its nature a man never hoards but always wants to share. The second thing is that joy is a mystery because it can happen anywhere, anytime, even under the most unpromising circumstances, even in the midst of suffering, with tears in its eyes. Even nailed to a tree."[41] Is your life moving in the one direction of joy?

"Open my eyes," the Psalmist prayed and pleaded with God. "Open my eyes that I may see wonderful things in your law" (Psalm 119:18,

41 Frederick Buechner, *Listening to Your Life: daily Meditations With Frederick Buechner*(New York: HarperCollins, 1992), 287.

NIV). This might not be a bad prayer in life's dung or daily devotions because it can bring tears to your eyes and joy to your heart. Open your eyes and open your heart to God's word and way; invite his grace in any circumstance.

I stumbled into an interesting tidbit of information in my office. I recognized the date: November 22, 1963. The late President John F. Kennedy lost his life to a sniper's bullet in Dallas on that day. C. S. Lewis died of cancer at his home in the Kilns on the outskirts of Headington Quarry, a residential village in Oxford, England. On the same day at 5:20 p.m. in Los Angeles, California, British author Aldous Leonard Huxley died of cancer of the tongue. Each wrote books. JFK wrote *Profiles in Courage*, a compilation of research and courageous acts from United States politicians. Lewis wrote several books like the children's set *The Chronicles of Narnia* and he had just completed his *Letters to Malcolm: Chiefly on Prayer*, published posthumously in 1964. Huxley penned *Brave New World* and *The Art of Seeing*. Huxley's book on *seeing* came in the aftermath of improved eyesight from a physician's new method for improving sight for those who had partial eyesight. Huxley's eyesight had been poor since he was a child.

The new medical method improved his sight and turned him in the light of a fresh direction.

So here is my question: Do you pray, "Open my eyes, Lord?" One man sees courage as the key to a noble life (Kennedy). Another sees images, sees abundance of life, see pulsating life in the creative wonder and work of Christ (Lewis). Another sees poorly, yet views life as meaningless, criticizes the materialists, describes in fiction his idea of utopias, and writes a book on *The Art of Seeing*. Each individually revealed their wounds, scars, hopes, and dreams in printed ink. What they wrote detailed what they saw in life. What do you see?

I asked twice in this chapter, "Did you see that?" Once I mentioned it discussing Paul's words about the fellowship of Christ's sufferings; another time talking about Joseph reconciling with his brothers in the goodness of forgiveness in the joyful tears of "God meant it for good." Did you see that? When we open our eyes to what God does by His grace, it increases the chances of our seeing His good, maturing in the bad, and sharing His grace with others as God's good things. Bad things turn to good things. You need only open your eyes, physically, daily, spiritually.

Someone asked me the other day, ""When you write, how do you come up with stuff?" Another person asked the question with an exclamation, "Where do you come up with this stuff!?" I pray. I sit. I put the ink to the paper, my fingers to the computer keys, and my wounds and scars I pour out in blood, sweat, and tears.

I never leave my library to write. I have saved stuff since I was nineteen years of age. Books line shelves. Stories of JFK, Lewis, Huxley, bones, eyes, wounds, scars, and a 116-year- old lady leap off of pages. Present-day writers, the living, and dead writers talk to me in books. I ponder. I pray. I think. I connect the dots. I write. I write some more. I listen. Bones speak.

Bones shout. Bones state their cases from the cold soil of the grave. I listen to God and write. I tell stories. Some days words collide like stars exploding in space, a glorious array of beauty. Some days I write and wish I were riding a moped on a garden isle, or climbing a mountain, or swimming the surf on some majestic beach. Mostly, I plod and write one word at a time.

Sometimes I lie in bed and think and write in my head. Occasionally, I watch the sunset on the back porch and think thoughts of wounds and scars, mopeds and tetanus shots, and faith and grace. I write as a wounded person under God's grace, wishing to heal your hurts as a wounded healer by ink. I like the connection. I like the power of joy leaping off of pages. I relish God's grace spilled in blood flowing as ink like a river into your heart.

Some days, and with this I must end this chapter, I arrive at thoughts in the drive-through line while waiting to arrive at the window to pick up my Chick fil A order. I hope, just hope, some saint has read my book about *Sacred Dung: Grace to Turn Bad Things Into Good Things.* I pray the readers like you have taken the book to heart. I pray we, the wounded healers by grace, heal others in Jesus's name. I pray that we the chaplains of the shadows shoot light like stars to pierce the darkness.

When I arrive at the window at Chick fil A, I hope, somehow, some way, some day on a porch swing you have read my book. I pray you were in front of me in the Chick fil A drive-through. And, pray tell, I wish you took the book to heart and paid for my meal. Because, deep down, we all know when God graces us, when He turns the bad things into good things, we spread His good news.

Our mourning turns to dancing. And we all know there is no joy like doing a good thing to spread joy in a wounded and hurting world.

"The person in front of you paid for your meal. Have a good day," the smiling server says through the window. "Yes! Yes, oh yes! Thank you, ma'am," I smile back. I shake my right arm in celebration like a baseball player who just won the MLB World Series. For when God's people graced do good things, the world swells with joy and it puts a glorious smile on faces everywhere.

Or better yet, I have taken the book to heart, and you are behind me in line at the drive- through at Chick fil A. I just paid for your meal! Yes, yes, oh yes! Passing along the good things, God's good things builds community, fellowship, and a feast of endless joy.

In my life, I choose the good things: kindness not meanness; God's grace, not un-grace; love not hate; forgiveness not bitterness; hope not hopelessness; grace not grumbling; and joy, not heckling madness in a world gone mad.

Conclusion

"When I understand that everything happening to me is to make me more Christlike, it solves a great deal of anxiety."

A. W. Tozer, from Pinterest

"It is doubtful whether God can bless a man greatly until he has hurt him deeply."

A. W. Tozer[42]

---

42 A. W. Tozer, *Fellowship of the Burning Heart* (ed. James L. Snyder; Alachua, Florida: Bridge-Logos, 2006), 16.

"Yea doubtless, and I count all things but loss for the excellency of the knowledge of Christ Jesus my Lord: for whom I have suffered the loss of all things, and do count them but dung, that I may win Christ..."

The Apostle Paul, Philippians 3:8, KJV

Write this down: This book soon ends; but your journey of grace renewed begins.

In the introduction, I told you the story of my friend, Jason Black. He wondered if he would ever sing again. By now you have read this book possibly reflecting on your own journey, your own spinouts, you own days stuck in the mud, your own wounds, scars, and days when you felt like dung.

In writing the book I found myself analyzing and considering you, your wounds, and your scars. At one point in writing, I stopped. I closed my eyes. I imagined Jesus on the cross. I watched Paul walk through the Roman world in sandals and a toga amid Roman oppression. I wondered what it must have been like for Nehemiah on his horse inspecting the Dung Gate, rebuilding the walls in Jerusalem among hardship, and then singing with the singer's words of praise after completion of the walls. I imagined Moses in the wilderness, his loneliness, prayers, wondering what God would do next in his life, and if he would make it out of his wilderness alive. I imagined Joseph in prison, in limbo, in pain, longing for home, and in reconciliation in the spirit of rejoicing at a banquet of forgiveness. I imagined and my mind drifted.

Harlem social activist and poet Langston Hughes (1902-1967), *jazz poetry* as he wrote, came to mind. It occurred to me our lives bounce around like a pinball in a pinball machine, up and down, back and forth. Hughes' personal, emotional pinball might describe our own, albeit in a different age, a different place, a different circumstance. He jazzes up hope: "We have tomorrow, Bright before us like a flame." He plays the notes of despair, dissonance of a life off-key: "Who cares about the hurt in your heart? Make a song like this for a jazz band to play: Nobody cares. Nobody cares." He sings of the trials of life: "Descent is quick. To rise again is slow."

He offers faith as an antidote to the poison of pain, as fertilizer to life's dung: "Sing, O Lord Jesus! Song is a strong thing. I heard my mother singing when life hurt her: Gonna rise in my chariot some day!"[43] Our lives bounce around from hope to despair to faith to trials and back to hope again. At times our lives feel bruised, wounded, scarred, and beat up by the existence of a bounce-around-pinball-life. At times our lives feel unsettled. I have written to you to offer hope in despair, faith in Christ in the trials, and grace as endurance and a healing ointment.

Almost twenty years ago, the late Calvin Miller and I shared a meal at Bennigan's, an Irish pub-themed casual restaurant. I met him at the seminary in Fort Worth. We drove in his red sports car. He showed me a finished manuscript from his book *Walking With the Angels*. I read an excerpt. He talked. I talked. At the time I faced challenges as a pastor in my eighth year at a church. I stayed twenty years in hope and joy under the great grace of God and his people.

Dr. Miller revealed to me stories of his own pastoral pain, his sometimes paranoia, and the night he showed up at prayer meeting to pray as church softball team members attempted to pray him out of the church. He later wrote about these times in his autobiography, *Life is Mostly Edges*.

---

43 Langston Hughes, *Langston Hughes: Poems* (New York: Alfred A. Knopf, 1994), 31, 63, 72, 96.

He unveiled stories walking with the angels, surviving those not-so-angelic demons, and God's grace dripped in the blood of joy. His infamous quote summarized the demons he faced at times as a pastor, "Paranoia has always been a problem of mine, but I had had enough church scrapes to know sometimes, when you think everyone is after you, they really are."[44] It never occurred to me that heroes hurt until that day.

I ate with Calvin on only two other occasions. One of those days he came to hear me preach. Another day he purchased a couple of his books, signed them, and gave them to me as a cherished gift. I learned from him of our hunger for meaning, spiritual meaning anchored in the grace of Christ. I also learned the importance of sitting before Jesus at a table of inwardness, clear focus on Christ. I further learned that even on life's dark, dreary days when life stinks like dung, you can still drink at Christ's table and savor a taste of joy. The joy is Christ.

One day while searching for a quote by another author in my office, I pulled a copy of Calvin Miller's *The Singer* off the shelf. I purchased this

---

44 Calvin Miller, *Life is Mostly Edges: A Memoir* (Nashville, Tennessee: Thomas Nelson, 2008), 243.

book after stocking shelves one day in my youth when I worked at a Christian bookstore. I opened the book. Whether a coincidence, a serendipity, or a moment of grace when God spoke and dripped His living water into my parched soul, I noticed this quote: "It is always much more difficult to sing when the audience has turned its back."[45]

My mind traveled back to the day at Bennigan's and the hurt of a hero. My spirit retraced the pinball-life quotes of Hughes from hope to despair to faith to trials and back to hope again. My heart jettisoned this cargo to you, reading with hurts, wounds, and scars. It's always hard to sing the joy of Jesus when the audience has turned its back, or worse yet, when you feel the audience has turned its back. Ask Jason. Ask Jesus. Ask Paul. Ask Nehemiah. Ask Moses. Ask Joseph.

Write this down: Bad things happen. Bad things happen to bad people. Bad things happen to good people. Good things happen to bad people. Good things happen to good people. Things happen. One day dung flies in your face, another day you step into it, and still another you find

---

45 Calvin Miller, *The Singer* (Downer's Grove, Illinois: InterVarsity Press, 1975), 43.

yourself feeling stuck in it, sniffing it like the smell of a skunk that nested in your house.

What Jesus teaches us, what Paul, Nehemiah, Moses, and Joseph discovered is that God always listens to your song and never turns His back. He hears your voice of lament or woe or prayer or hope or gasped words of uncertainty in the deep sighs of longing for certainty in the weariness of long days. God is faithful to hear. God is faithful to hear you. God is faithful when you feel the audience has turned its back.

I cannot speak for you, but I feel in my own life that I have had to learn to sing God's song of joy again. Rejoice in the Lord, again I say rejoice (Philippians 4:4). Or rejoice in the Lord always, again I say, rejoice (Philippians 4:4). Again we understand. Always often proves challenging, especially when the audience has turned its back, your critics have amped up the volume, or you find yourself knee-high in dung in your bathroom after a hard rain when the septic has backed up in your house.

At the age of five, one of my daughters tossed her toy from her McDonald's Happy Meal into the toilet. You do not have to be a rocket scientist to guess what happened: the toilet stopped up full of wet toilet paper and dung, the water overflowed, and this non-rocket scientist had to attempt plumbing. Up to my knees in dung, one mess, one plunger, and one prayer, Lord, help me, later, the toy retrieved, the toilet flowed freely again. That day does not go down on my calendar as one for the ages. However, I will never forget it. I never enjoyed it.

If the Greek philosopher Plato (429-347 B.C.) proves right in his theory that life's real creator, it appears, will be our needs, or as it is often translated, "Necessity is the mother of invention," then necessity of the dung calls for creativity.[46] If your daughter plugs up the toilet and you find yourself deep in the dung, literally, be creative. A plunger and a hanger did the trick for me. If, figuratively, your life has backed up and you find yourself wet and stuck in dung, this calls for the Creator, God in the wonder of His grace. He will creatively clear the pathways, open the lines, and create a free flow of grace to make your life work again. He will assist you and free you to sing again.

Whether you sing aloud in the bathroom, in the shower, on stage, or in the streets again

---

46 Plato, *The Republic II*.369C.

remains your choice. But His grace will free your soul to sing His joy again, always.

So how does God's grace set you free when the dung rises in your life? Write this down: Everybody in life at one time or another needs a dung gate. Clear out the past. Trash the unwanted stuff, sin, negativity, and pain of the past. Do not forget it, but neither let it dirty up your soul. Sacred refuse trashed frees up space in your heart for God's freshness.

Write this down: One day you will wake up in the dark wilderness and it will be just what the doctor ordered. I am in Arabia now, in a wilderness of sorts, but I am opening my eyes to God's grandeur. I look around and see cactus, a lone flower, birds overhead, blue skies, and a glorious sunset on the distant horizon. I recognize that the Creator creatively, even miraculously, helps His servants find a path out of the wilderness. The God of grace aided by His grace, Nehemiah, Moses, Joseph, Paul, provides a way out for all of us in Jesus Christ. The dung can be destroyed in the wilderness if only you will look to Christ, consider dung as temporary, focus on the Eternal, and allow the dung of the wilderness to fertilize your soul for future days.

A sacred refrain might slow your life down. It might make you wonder, "What's coming next?" A refrain that embraces God's sacred might force you to depend on God by faith, and for seeds to germinate in the soil and dung of your soul, because God intends that soul to bear fruit in you in future days. Remember this? Jesus gives a kind of humorous play on words: dung (*kopron*) is necessary for you to bear fruit (*karpon*). So I offer you this formula: Add *kopron* to your life in Christ to bear *karpon*. Or Jesus plus a little dung helps you bear fruit in God's kingdom. Or better yet, a little dung never hurt anyone. After all, dung, like a wilderness experience, can actually be good for the soul. A sacred refrain might be just what God in his creative handiwork ordered to bless you.

Write this down: Your pain is not your own. Of all the words spoken, words written, and words penned in ink, these words might sound strange. You enter into Christ's suffering. He suffers with you because He Himself has suffered, understands, and comforts us in our suffering. The dung matures us, so to speak; and, like the doctors of the prominent Roman naval commander, equestrian, and writer Pliny the Elder (A.D. 23-79) prescribed, the dung rubbed on our wounds heals us.

Once healed by God's grace, we then seek to heal and help the hurt in others' lives.

Even heroes hurt. Each person hurts so open your eyes. Be a person of grace. Live in compassion. Be kind for the burdens people carry often go unseen. Serve Christ by soothing others. Serve Christ by serving others. Serve Christ by sharing grace.

Sacred refuse and a sacred refrain invite us to seek God as our sacred refuge. We seek God our refuge; find strength in Him by grace; and become a safe refuge for others to heal from their hurts, wounds, and scars.

When we embrace the sacred even in life's dung, when we encounter God's grace as sacred in the darkness, when we expect God's grace to work in us and on our behalf in the wilderness of the dung, then sacred dung becomes a time, place, and refuge to lengthen and strengthen our faith.

In my office I stumbled into another story. I say *stumbled* because I piled several newspaper clippings in a pile for the trash. Get rid of the dung on trash day, right? If you do not get rid of the dung, you're done. Did I say that?

The story comes with a book: *Fall To Grace*. The story caught my attention with an Associated

Press headline: "Stained by scandal, Bliss back in coaching at Okla. School." The story swirls with drama: a Baylor University men's basketball player kills his teammate and buries him in a dump yard, a trash heap, a dung heap. While Coach Dave Bliss had nothing to do with the murder, the investigation of the murder led to revelations of rule-breaking, improper tuition payments, and a scandal no less filled with stench like the day my toilet backed up.

In 2003 Coach Bliss resigned his coaching job at Baylor, woke up in the dung, and in a wilderness of self-doubt in a fall from grace. One day with the help of friends, he carried his past to the Dung Gate, renewed his life with Christ in the wilderness, and leaped into the future, in his own words, to see "what God can do with my story," to help others both avoid his mistakes and learn from his mistakes.

He now coaches men's basketball at seventy-one years of age at a small Christian college in Bethany, Oklahoma. The athletic director proclaimed Bliss a man transformed (by Christ) and redeemed (by grace) in need of a second chance. Bliss' book details the journey: revelation, exodus, wilderness, and the promise (or God's promises;

land of promise). Bliss coached, then resigned, then worried about the future in the wilderness, discovered the grace of a second chance in life after he bounced around like a pinball in a pinball machine, up and down, back and forth. Bliss's fall from grace wounded and scarred him until he fell into God's grace ready to serve Christ in the joy of a second chance.

God majors in communion that sets us on the right path, community that sets us free among people, and compassion demonstrated by Him and by His grace-filled servants. All told for Coach Bliss, he was not done in the dung because he yielded his *kopron* of his life in Christ to bear *karpon*. Surely you have this down by now: the dung bears fruit in the soil of God's grace.

So here I am. Dark clouds build in puffy whiteness and blueness. The weatherman calls for storms, driving rain, hail that will pound your automobile, and thunder that will pound your heart. I am in my office looking around at books, through the window the clouds, and I have my eyes wide open. "Open my eyes," the Psalmist prayed. I am praying that in my own life right now.

For some unknown reason, my mind drifts from my office to the mountains of North Carolina.

This actually happened years ago. I remember. I am a young man. I sit on the porch in a green swing. I read Frederick Buechner's, *Beyond Words*. I have never met Buechner but I like him. He lives in Vermont. His living bones speak. He says, "If the new is to be born, though, the old has to die. It is the law of the place. For the best to happen, the worst must stop happening-the worst we are, the worst we do."[47] I am on the porch as thunder rumbles over the mountains in North Carolina. Buechner in Vermont and me on the porch reading, the thunder rolls.

Rain starts falling. My grandmother hoes in the garden in the light rain. She wears an apron, a bonnet, wedges the dirt with a hoe, and drops beans, cabbage, and corn in a white bucket with a silver handle. Obviously, the rich soil fertilized bore fruit both fresh and nutritional. I watch my grandmother work. In her early eighties at the time, I figure she has enough sense to know when to get in out of the rain.

The thunder rolls over the hills. The rain pours like someone opened the floodgates at Hoover Dam. The rain then dives, drives, and

---

47 Frederick Buechner, *Beyond Words: Daily Reading in the ABCs of Faith* (New York: Harper Collins, 2004), 149.

swirls in the air, the mist swirling in the wind like the hovering mists of Niagara Falls. The thunder rattles the windows. I keep reading. I am beyond words. Buchner's words suddenly rattle my bones: "The grace of God means something like: 'Here is your life. You might never have been, but you are, because the party wouldn't have been complete without you. Here is the world. Beautiful and terrible things happen. Don't be afraid. I am with you. Nothing can separate us. It's for you I created the universe. I love you.'"[48]

My grandmother has enough sense to get in out of the rain. She carries the bucket, walks from the garden through the yard to the porch, steps up, enters the front door, and the screen door slams shut as she enters the house. The rain falls, harder, faster, louder, much like life at times. Later she returns. The door slightly opened, she looks at me with grace.

"Supper's ready," she says in her apron minus her bonnet. I enter the house, sit at the table, and the feast unfolds: vegetables, fruit, fresh from the garden. Joy swirls like the mist of Niagara, fresh on my face, fresh in my heart.

---

48 Buechner, *Beyond Words*, 139.

I am back now. My grandmother has been in heaven for almost twenty years. Her bones still speak. They rattle my bones and speak to me. She loved the Psalms. We read one every night at her house in the mountains. We read Psalms like this one: "You are the most excellent of men and your lips have been anointed with grace, since God has blessed you forever" (Psalm 45:2, NIV). Compassionate, it sounds like something she might have spoken, "Most precious man, woman, you are blessed. Your lips are anointed with grace." Yes, her bones still speak: "We are saved by grace to live by grace to share his grace."

Write this down: Sacred dung means that bad things can turn to good things when touched by God's grace. Write this down: Beautiful and horrible things happen. Grace happens, too. Write this down: Do not be afraid, neither should you wallow in the dung. Write this down: Everybody needs a dung gate. Write this down: One day you will wake up in the dark wilderness and it will be just what the doctor ordered. Write this down: Your pain is not your own.

I cannot tell you what God is doing or wants to do in your life, but what I can say is this: you're done in the dung, mired there if you do not surrender it to God's amazing grace. But you'll find joy in his grace if you let the dung bear fruit in you. You have it down now, don't you? Dung, the Dung Gate, dung as fertilizer, dung as grace to heal your wounds so that you can heal and help others? You remembered, huh? Add *kopron* to your life in Christ to bear *karpon*.

You've got it, huh, sacred dung? God's grace turns bad things into good things. So write this down: His grace is sufficient for you. His grace is made perfect in weakness. His grace fertilizes the soil of your soul so that you can bear fruit in future days. I knew you would get it: Add kopron to your life in Christ to bear karpon.

Good night. Let it rain. Let the thunder roll. Let the windows rattle. Listen for the bones that speak to rattle your soul. Let his grace fall fresh on you. Good night. Do not forget to turn out the light. Did you lock the door? Can you hear the rain falling on the roof? Let His grace fall fresh like rain on you. I feel the mist on my face; do you? The mist of grace?

A "Sacred Triology"

by John Duncan

Order the complete set at

www.austinbrotherspublishing.com

John D. Duncan

Sacred Space

The Art of Sacred Silence,
Sacred Speech, and
The Sacred Ear
in the Echo of the
Still Small Voice of God

John D. Duncan

Sacred Grit

Faith to Push Through
When You Feel
Like Giving Up

Foreword by Charles Breithaupt

John D. Duncan

Sacred Dung

Grace to Turn
Bad Things
Into Good Things

CPSIA information can be obtained
at www.ICGtesting.com
Printed in the USA
FSOW02n2242120815
9643FS